Praise for the book

"The book describes the role of procurement in corporations. It shows how people in procurement should jointly work with business departments to bring value to their company.

The usual approach of people in procurement is simply to put pressure on vendors to decrease prices and force vendors to accept tough penalties. In contrast to that simplistic approach, the author shows that working with a vendor to come to a good balanced solution is a long and complex process.

Selling large contracts to corporations requires knowledge, business culture and experience. Selling processes are long, go through different phases, have ups and downs at all stages, involve decision makers at various levels of purchaser and vendor management hierarchies. Selling according to B2B model demands a lot of skills and knowledge on the selling side. The book presents that knowledge in a very well-structured manner."

—Janusz Filipiak, Founder and CEO of Comarch, a software company that employs nearly 5000 people in 26 countries and author of 6 books.

"Literally every page had something of interest to us – sometimes it was a table, an anecdote, or even an innocuous one-sentence quip – but the information on each page is truly helpful to the owner of a business like mine, which is trying to sell to larger organizations.

Should our business ever grow in such a way that we would be the ones needing to procure goods or services, or should we ever hire someone to do the procurement for us – this may sound slightly pretentious, but I feel that upon reading this book – I could end up doing a better job in a procurement capacity than people I know who do it for a living. This book is simply chock-full of incredible advice from the first page to the last."

—Michael Glazer, CEO of Premier Service Inc. a Canadian-based mystery shopping and engagement company co-founded in 1991

"In my field of business, the sales process has often been focused on target customers, segmentation and need analysis, and identifying unique value proposition. I see adding a better understanding of the role of the purchasing department, its objectives, and relationship with stakeholders as a key factor in achieving a successful sales strategy.

The accuracy of the content mirrors and relates easily to what I have experienced in the field. The structure has a logical flow and makes it easy to read. I have not been in disagreement with any points mentioned in the book."

—Yan Bergeron, Sales Director at PixMob Middle East Africa Turkey. Yan has spent 8 years working in one of the largest IT companies in the world.

CONFESSIONS OF A PROFESSIONAL BUYER

THE SECRETS ABOUT SELLING & PURCHASING SERVICES

By

HUBERT LACHANCE

Author:

Hubert Lachance

hlachance@hotmail.com

Front cover city background:

"Thiago Leite/Shutterstock.com"

ISBN: 978-0-995286412

First Edition: September 2016

ACKNOWLEDGEMENTS

This book was made possible thanks to the collaboration of many people.

I would like to thank my senior procurement colleagues, who have provided constructive feedback to enhance this book. They have significantly contributed to building my expertise and becoming a better procurement professional.

Special thanks to Manon Campbell, Procurement Business Manager, Patrick Aussant, Manager Strategic Sourcing and Louis Boucher.

I am grateful to Denis Bourgeault, Vice President Operations, at Umano Medical Inc. for awarding me with my first Procurement job in Direct Procurement. Thanks to Martin Michaud, Martine Chouinard and Dominic Savard, who have provided guidance when I started in Procurement.

Thanks to Michael Landou for the nice cover.

I would like to thank those who have participated in the feedback process.

Rick Cleveland, Director of Education and Accreditation for the Supply Chain Management Association of Canada (SCMA)

Janusz Filipiak, CEO and founder of Comarch & Łukasz Słoniewski, Consulting Director at Comarch

Christine S. Filip, Esq., owner of Business Development Partners

Yan Bergeron, Sales Director, PixMob Middle East Africa Turkey

Michael Glazer, CEO of Premier Service Inc.

Pierre Gignac, President of MPG Modular Products Group Inc. / X-Lite Canada Inc.

CHAPTERS DETAILED OVERVIEW

Section 1: Sourcing Context

Chapter 1: Sourcing Services

This chapter explains the differences between direct and indirect procurement. It covers widely used procurement terminologies such as RFQs (Request For Quotations), RFPs (Request for Proposals) and RFIs (Request for Information).

Some of the main challenges associated with sourcing/selling indirect categories are presented. The chapter concludes by illustrating the optimal procurement involvement sequence with some statistics on sourcing coverage.

Chapter 2: Why Corporations Hire Buyers

This chapter helps strategic purchasers understand their roles. This information will allow sales professionals to recognize common areas of interest and understand some of procurement's challenges.

Chapter 3: Challenges of Acquiring New Customers

This chapter explains the challenges that sales professionals face when looking for new customers and when purchasers are dealing with new suppliers. This knowledge will allow all stakeholders (buyers, entrepreneurs, sales representatives, budget holders, and suppliers) to understand the strategies aimed at maximizing sourcing/selling outcomes.

Section 2

Chapter 4: Maximizing the Outcomes of Strategic Sourcing Processes

This chapter presents the important steps of the strategic sourcing process. This knowledge will allow indirect purchasers to lead indirect sourcing initiatives.

For sales professionals, understanding the strategic sourcing process will help achieve better outcomes when answering tender requests (RFPs and RFQs). Strategies to convince customers to limit RFPs frequencies will be presented.

Chapter 5: Managing Gifts & Entertainment

This chapter explains basic rules related to gifts and entertainment.

Chapter 6: How to Maintain Existing Customers

This chapter summarizes some of the strategies that sales professionals can leverage to retain existing customers and strengthen partnerships.

Conclusion

The conclusion offers a high level overview of the key learning.

TABLE OF CONTENT

INTRODUCTION

This book is intended for all stakeholders involved in the process of selling and purchasing indirect goods and services.

It is a well-known fact that procurement involvement in indirect acquisitions is increasing. In order to respond to this new trend, the author, an expert in indirect procurement with more than 10 years of professional experience, reveals secrets to selling and purchasing services from the procurement's perspective.

Readers will have a chance to further their knowledge about purchaser's roles and understand how large companies handle their sourcing process. This knowledge will help readers gain a new perspective about the possibilities of leveraging relationships between purchasers and suppliers.

Sales professionals will learn how to reach their objectives of securing new clients and promoting repetitive business. Answering RFP's will no longer be a secret.

Purchasers, who are new to acquiring services, will understand the dynamics and processes associated with sourcing indirect categories. This knowledge will allow them to feel at ease to lead and obtain enhanced value from their assigned sourcing projects.

The author presents the information in six revealing and in-depth chapters:

- Sourcing services
- Why corporations hire buyers
- Challenges of acquiring new customers
- Maximizing outcomes of strategic sourcing processes
- Managing gifts and entertainment
- How to maintain existing customers

ABOUT THE AUTHOR

Hubert Lachance was born in Quebec, Canada and now lives in Montreal, sharing a house with his mother-in-law, wife, and three children. He obtained an MBA in International Business in 2004, as well as a BAA in 2002, from Laval University and participated in two student exchange programs, one in the United States and one in Mexico. These helped him to understand how different cultures affect and influence businesses.

He has worked for more than 10 years for a well-known international consumer packaged goods company. His past position as a Sourcing Associate involved acquiring services (indirect procurement) for marketing, IT, and corporate affairs. Hubert has also experienced sourcing goods (direct procurement) when negotiating major purchasing contracts for an American-owned hospital bed manufacturer.

Throughout his career as a buyer, Hubert has had the opportunity to work with many companies (suppliers), offering a wide range of products and services. As a result, Hubert is in a privileged position to share hands-on information on many topics related to B2B from a procurement's perspective.

STRUCTURE OF THE BOOK

First section

Readers will learn or review basic procurement terminologies and understand the particulars of acquiring/selling services. The purchasers' roles will be presented, followed by a review of the numerous challenges of acquiring new indirect customers. This information will allow leveraging the relationships between suppliers and purchasers.

Sourcing Context:

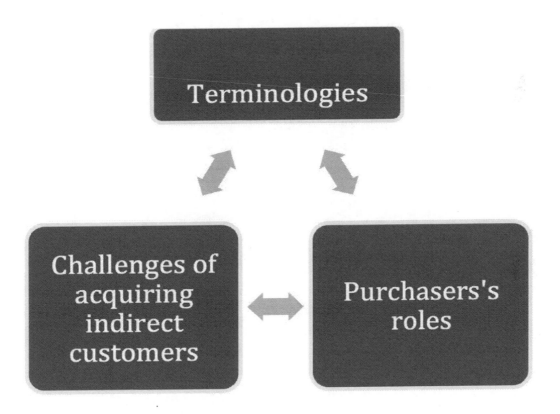

Figure 1

Second section

The second section covers the strategic sourcing process that is divided into 9 phases. The knowledge from this section will allow purchasers and sales professionals to maximize the outcomes of each phase.

Strategic sourcing process overview:

1) Needs identification

2) Market analysis

3) Purchasing strategies

4) Market approaches

5) Proposal presentations

6) Suppliers' selection and negotiations

7) Supplier's feedback

8) Purchase order/contract

9) Suppliers' evaluation

The delicate topic of gifts and entertainment will be presented, with a comprehensive list of all actions aimed at retaining existing customers.

INTRODUCTORY EXAMPLE

Before reviewing some basic definitions related to sourcing services, let's kick off with an introductory example. This past experience explains where the idea of writing this book came from and illustrates some of the challenges associated with indirect acquisitions.

A couple of years ago, I got involved toward the end of an upcoming web application deal that had been negotiated by a budget holder. At that time, procurement was still struggling to get a seat at the table, and it seemed that we were the only ones focused on controlling costs.

At the outset of my involvement with the pending deal, my first impression was that we were being taken to the cleaners. To confirm my assumption, I performed a quick benchmarking exercise during which I was told that the normal cost was roughly twenty times lower than what my internal client was about to pay. One may think that this was a great opportunity to show procurement's value and gain support. The reality was that the more the budget holder was challenged, the more resistance I faced. I was told that I did not understand the complexity of the service, yet it was extremely difficult to obtain any details.

After two months of struggling to gain more information, I was finally able to ask for formal quotations. It turns out that the cost really was twenty times lower. Even after sharing this information, it was still difficult to align with my internal stakeholders.

Through internal enquiries, I was told that the supplier had asked what the budget was and quoted accordingly. That supplier was not flexible at all during negotiations, because he felt protected by the budget holder.

While working with another supplier who ended up with the contract, I gradually developed a better relationship with the sales representative. This individual has explained that he was skilled and managed to secure business with us. Although I believe that he was highly skilled, I also knew that his company got selected, mainly because their bid was 20 times lower than what we were about to pay.

This sales professional clearly had a different perspective on how he managed to secure a contract with our company. This incident made me believe that it would be interesting for buyers to share their side of the story, while offering a learning opportunity for sales professionals and other buyers.

CHAPTER 1: SOURCING SERVICES

This chapter explains the differences between direct and indirect procurement. It covers widely used procurement terminologies such as RFQs (Request For Quotations), RFPs (Request for Proposals) and RFIs (Request for Information).

Some of the main challenges associated with sourcing/selling indirect categories are presented. The chapter concludes by illustrating the optimal procurement involvement sequence with some statistics on sourcing coverage. We will start by laying out of the definitions:

DIRECT PROCUREMENT IS DEFINED AS

The "purchase of goods and services that are directly incorporated into a product being manufactured or a service provided to the end customer (or public)."[1] For example, for an automobile manufacturer, automotive parts are considered direct material.

INDIRECT PROCUREMENT CAN BE DEFINED AS

The purchases of goods and services that are necessary for a company to operate. These purchases are usually made on behalf of a budget holder and are not directly associated with production.

The following list from Procurement Leaders [2] presents the different indirect categories:

- Facilities management
- IT
- HR
- Marketing
- Logistics
- Printing and packaging
- Professional services
- Telecommunications
- Travel and fleet
- Energy and utilities
- Maintenance, repairs and operations (MRO)

Distinctions Between RFP, RFQ & RFI

As per its title, the focus of this book is to explain how to maximize the outcome of requests for proposals by experiencing each step that professional purchasers follow. In the context of acquiring indirect goods and services, RFPs are more frequently used than RFQs.

Since requirements are less strict in an RFP than in an RFQ, it leaves more opportunities for sales professionals who have the proper skills potentially to influence the outcome of a tender process.

Below are presented the definitions of RFP, RFQ and RFI:

RFP Definition

A RFP (request for proposal) is a bidding solicitation to multiple organizations. RFPs typically allow for certain flexibility in terms of recommended solutions to address needs that are often challenging to communicate. In order to evaluate which proposal addresses better the requirements, buyers rely on a set of selection criteria and price is often not the primary one. When sourcing indirect categories, the "decision maker is the internal client (most often a budget holder), and procurement plays an advisory role." [3]

To simplify explanations, I will refer most of the time to a budget holder as being the internal client. In reality, it could also be an employee working for a budget holder, or other internal decision makers involved in the acquisition process.

RFQ Definition

A RFQ (request for quotation) could be summarized as a bidding solicitation where multiple companies are being asked to quote on strict set of requirements. Price is one of the main decision criteria when technical requirements and delivery can be met. Strict requirements are usually provided by technical experts such as engineers and cannot be easily changed.

In some instances, the requirements or manufacturing parts are certified by public authorities, such as FDA (Food and Drug Administration), FAA (Federal Aviation Administration), and TC (Transport Canada) etc.

Since requirements are clearly communicated in RFQs, purchasers are usually the ones selecting suppliers. RFQs are predominantly used when sourcing direct material (also called goods for resale).

RFI Definition

An RFI (request for information) is another form of solicitation that is used to understand what the market has to offer and improve knowledge of products, services and suppliers. Typically, price is not the main focus of an RFI, although estimates can be provided. Generally, an RFP or an RFQ follows an RFI, should the company decide to move ahead with its sourcing initiative. RFIs are very important, because the information gained can become requirements, thus enabling participants to become closer to securing a contract.

Evolution of the sourcing context

Historically, the main focus of procurement has been on reducing prices of raw material and purchased components. Large companies have invested in ERP systems capable of tracking cost of all items included in their production. Given high volumes of components associated with manufacturing production, the impact of price reductions is known to directly influence companies' bottom lines.

In this context, the contribution of purchasers specialized in direct procurement is well recognized.

In response to the growing importance of the service sector in industrialized economies and the challenges of continually reducing prices for direct goods, large companies are gradually putting more emphasis on indirect spending.

Whereas suppliers used to deal directly with budget holders, they are now more likely than before to deal with procurement. In most large companies, indirect expenses represent significant investments that deserve proper support from procurement. Although indirect savings are usually invested in acquiring additional services rather than directly impacting company's bottom lines, they definitely contribute to improving financial wealth and efficiency.

CHALLENGES ASSOCIATED WITH SOURCING/SELLING INDIRECT CATEGORIES

Sourcing/selling indirect goods and services represent a challenge for many professionals. From the purchasing side, one of the main challenges is for budget holders and purchasers to define requirements without necessarily being experts in all categories.

A good example of the challenge of drafting requirements would be an IT project leader and a buyer involved in sourcing MFP (multi-function printers). Chances are that both are not experts in drafting MFP's specifications. Relying too much on a supplier for support could make the sourcing process unfair.

On the other side, not being as precise as an engineer drafting specifications is not necessarily negative; being too precise could limit solutions that may exceed expectations. Another challenge is to understand which selection criteria should be used to properly select the best proposal when price is not usually the main one.

On the selling side, having the possibility of supplying an appropriate offer is often not enough to secure orders. A first challenge is to manage to meet with decision makers, understand precisely what they are looking for and earn their confidence. Without a proper approach, new suppliers are likely to fall short over existing service providers that had the opportunity to better understand requirements and develop relationships.

The previously mentioned challenges only represent a portion of what stakeholders will have to deal with when purchasing/selling indirect goods and services. The next chapters provide comprehensive explanations of these challenges and more.

IDEAL PROCUREMENT INVOLVEMENT SEQUENCE

In this section we will review the optimal procurement involvement sequence. For any purchases that qualify for a sourcing process, it is important that procurement be involved at the right moment.

The time to involve procurement is when drafting requirements. Involving procurement at a later stage usually reduces buyers' contribution and could lead to unfair situations for suppliers quoting on a project.

As an example, if procurement is only involved when it is time to place a purchase order, how could a buyer suggest alternatives and have enough leverage to negotiate? Below is presented the optimal involvement sequence.

Optimal Involvement Sequence:

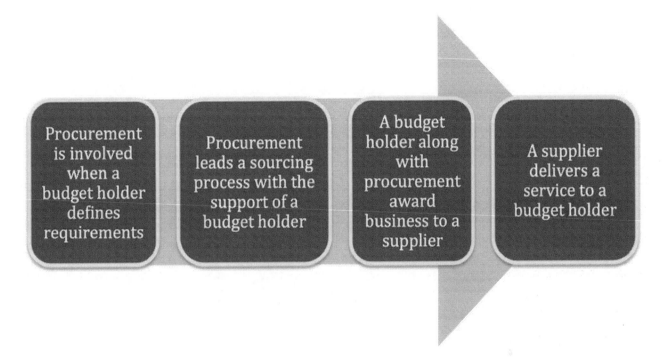

Figure 2

When budget holders and procurement manage to work together and follow this simple sequence they can obtain the following benefits.

Benefits of This Sequence:

- Receiving a number of different proposals allows for negotiation and selection of the optimal solution through enhanced knowledge.

- Faster to source; carefully defining needs and/or expectations allows for a tender process to occur with less ongoing correspondence with suppliers.

- Procurement can contribute to the needs identification phase, thus recommending innovative solutions.

- Increased chances for a fair sourcing process, since procurement has to follow a strict selection process.

Non-Ideal Sourcing Sequence (When Buyers are Involved Too Late in the Process):

The non-ideal sourcing sequence is common when an indirect procurement is new in supporting indirect acquisitions.

The dynamic that often occurs is that a budget holder defines needs in collaboration with a supplier over a long period of time. When the project becomes urgent, procurement is being asked to approve a quotation and is left with a day or two to approve a purchase order. In this scenario, a budget holder would generally prefer not having to involve procurement at all, in order to move forward with a project and honour agreed commitments

Non-Ideal Sequence:

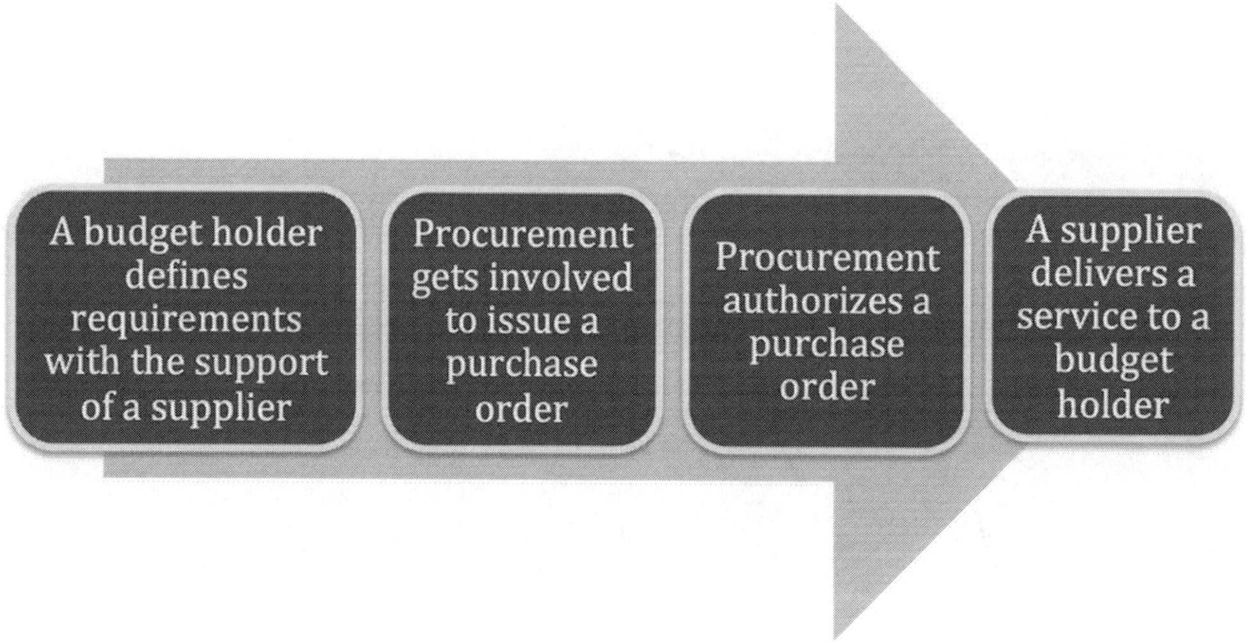

A budget holder defines requirements with the support of a supplier → Procurement gets involved to issue a purchase order → Procurement authorizes a purchase order → A supplier delivers a service to a budget holder

Figure 3

Inconveniences of This Purchasing Sequence:

- No options, only one supplier is involved

- Higher risk for inflated costs (up to twenty times normal cost!)

- A lot of time is spent deciphering requirements, much back and forth is necessary

- Suppliers may get blamed for non-delivery due to ever-changing requirements

- Procurement is not in a good position to negotiate or add commercial obligations that were not discussed right from the beginning

- Procurement is seen as and feels useless

- Suddenly adding new suppliers toward the end of a sourcing project is likely to be unfair for new bidders

Some suppliers may take advantage and overcharge customers that face this non-ideal scenario. When a buyer is uncertain of the situation, the recommendation is to do a benchmarking exercise and only intervene when necessary.

Although it is said that procurement must be involved from the outset, the reality is that indirect purchasers are not always involved at the right moment and sometimes they are not involved at all. Sourcing coverage (the percentage of spending influenced by procurement) for indirect categories is a challenge for many organizations and procurement involvement varies according to the indirect categories.

Which Indirect Categories do Procurement Influence? [4]

The following chart from Proxima, a leading procurement services provider, illustrates that indirect categories have an impact on procurement's influence (coverage).

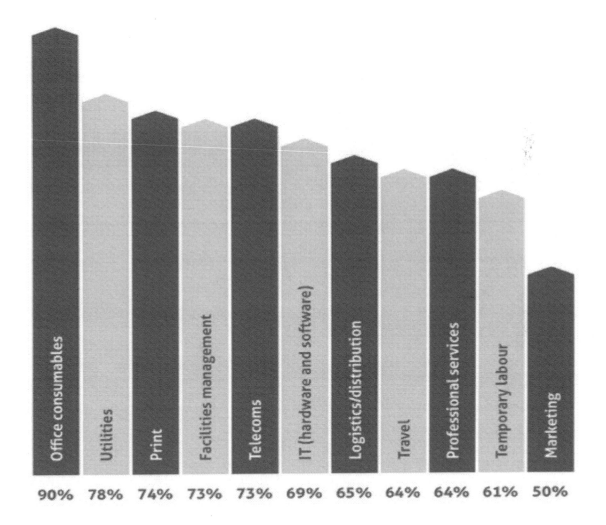

Figure 4

This information is relevant, because it gives an idea of the likelihood of procurement getting involved. Even when procurement is not involved, proactive suppliers can seek buyers' involvement. As we will see later on, this may be an effective strategy for potential new suppliers to manage to participate in an RFP.

As per the chart, marketing is an area where indirect purchasers struggle the most at influencing with only 50%. This illustrates what I have outlined already: that procurement is not always involved when they should be.

There are several reasons procurement is variably involved in sourcing indirect categories, particularly for marketing. One of them is that procurement involvement in marketing purchases is still quite recent. According to an survey conducted in 2013 [5], procurement has been involved in marketing purchases for only nine years.

CHAPTER 1 TAKEWAYS

- Given a different sourcing context, purchasers generally specialize either in direct or indirect purchases. Supporting indirect purchases is relatively new compared with direct purchases.

- RFPs are predominantly used to source indirect categories (services); price is not necessarily the main decision criterion, and solutions are likely to vary from one supplier to another. Various stakeholders are likely to participate in establishing requirements for indirect categories. Indirect purchasers usually play an advisory role in regards to suppliers' selection.

- RFQs are predominantly used to source direct material (goods for resale); price is one of the main decision criteria, and requirements are strict and provided by technical specialists. Direct purchasers are usually the ones handling commercial discussions with suppliers and deciding on which supplier to choose.

- Sourcing/selling indirect goods and services is challenging as it involves many stakeholders with different knowledge and expertise. Personal relationships can sometimes influence purchasing decisions, thus making it harder for new bidders. This book addresses these two main challenges and more.

- The time to involve procurement is when needs are being developed through collaboration between a purchaser and its internal client (budget holder). Involving procurement at a later stage generally reduces procurement contributions.

- The indirect category has an impact on procurement's influence, but buyers can support all indirect categories.

Chapter 2: Why Corporations Hire Buyers

This chapter helps strategic purchasers understand their roles. This information will allow sales professionals to recognize common areas of interest and understand some of procurement's challenges.

Overseeing the Acquisition Process

Everyone feels they have the capacity to make purchases for themselves. As a result, it can be challenging for procurement to lead indirect sourcing initiatives with new stakeholders. However, this does not give stakeholders the authority to act as purchasing representatives. When acquiring for medium and large size corporations, there are more rules to follow than when buying for oneself. In addition, there are systems in place and processes to follow. Due to the complexity and responsibilities involved, it is important to have a procurement function.

Ensuring that a Fair Process is in Place

The stronger a purchasing department is, the less chance there is that external stakeholders use their influence to alter sourcing decisions. This is a good reason having a strong procurement function is important, as it ensures the sourcing process is fair.

It is procurement's task to remind budget holders that there is no point in doing an RFP or an RFQ if new suppliers do not stand a chance of getting selected. Internal resistance is more frequent with indirect purchases.

Unfortunately, I cannot say that purchasing decisions are always entirely fair from a supplier's standpoint. When important transition costs (total cost of ownership) are discovered during a tender process, it will likely impact final outcomes. This means, even the most competitive supplier, as per the quotations received, may not win an RFP.

For example, in an RFP to source multi-function printers, I found out, toward the end of the sourcing process, the current supplier had the right to charge to dispose of the old equipment. Renewing the contract with this supplier would facilitate negotiating this aspect. In this same project, I was also informed that a significant investment would be required to develop compatibility software if we were to award the contract to a different supplier. These two elements made us decide to remain with the same supplier, although prices related to their printers were more expensive.

Supplier's Screening and Recommendations

Similar to an HR department that filters candidates, procurement screens suppliers to make acquisitions more efficient. Buyers want to work with the best and most reliable suppliers.

When an internal client is looking at acquiring products or services, they can usually rely on their procurement department to recommend trusted suppliers. As buyers represent many internal clients, they usually have more leverage in encouraging suppliers to deal with issues promptly.

To remain a supplier that procurement recommends, it is important to always deliver. From my experience, most suppliers are able to deliver according to an agreed timeline, but large corporations often face internal delays that suppliers may be asked to absorb.

Sometimes, it is not possible to absorb delays, and projects fall behind schedule. From my experience, internal clients will complain to procurement when they are not aware of timeline issues. Suppliers who are good at communicating their time constraints manage to avoid such complaints. I have seen suppliers who think they have to say yes to all requests for modifications, and then hope they will be able to deliver. This is a big mistake as sometimes, internal clients are picky and cannot make up their mind. When this occurs, the constant back and forth of e-mails can increase the risk of mistakes and delays.

The best way to avoid this unpleasant and risky scenario is by taking the proper time to analyze the impact of modifications and informing customers. If the internal client realizes that a slight change may delay his project by two months, he may become less picky!

SUPPLIER'S MAIN POINT OF CONTACT

Suppliers can count on purchasers to be their first point of contact to discuss topics, such as assessing business potential, bidding opportunities, late payments, payment terms, contracts, supplier performance, action plans, innovation, process improvements, issues, delays, commercial offers etc.

Personally, I like it when suppliers contact me when they cannot reach their internal client (budget holder), and they have to act immediately in order not to delay their projects. This shows that suppliers will do whatever it takes to deliver. It is generally easier for procurement to get a hold of a budget holder than it is for a supplier.

INNOVATION

Buyers have a privileged position within companies and are exposed to innovative ideas from suppliers often developing their own sense of curiosity. Although not all buyers have realized it yet, they are expected to contribute to the innovation process.

I have often heard purchasers from other companies complaining that their internal clients have visited suppliers or have attended tradeshows without their involvement. Companies need to evolve, and if procurement is not supportive, prospecting for innovation is likely to be conducted without them. Understanding that fostering innovation is an important procurement role, entrepreneurs and sales representatives can appreciate the opportunity that it presents.

Introducing Innovative Products/Services

Entrepreneurs that have innovative products or services certainly have a hard time triggering interest from procurement. One of the reasons for this is that procurement generally issues tenders based on existing needs. When suppliers come up with new ideas, it can be a challenge for procurement to assess whether the offer is reasonably priced. When innovative ideas appear to be fairly priced and cost can be easily forecasted, it helps to get procurement supportive of promoting the idea of trying something new to budget holders. When a potential customer is not willing to try something new, offering a free pilot could be considered. I have seen great business ideas never materialize, because companies are used to the tried and true. Furthermore, customers do not embrace piloting new ideas at their own expense.

When presenting new ideas, it is recommended that you remain flexible on how the services can be rendered. For example, the prospective customer may only like a portion of what you are offering. Being too stubborn and ignoring requests for modifications may mean you lose out.

Technical professionals, with no sales background, often have issues when selling their revolutionary products, because they tend to focus on the technical capabilities. Purchasers are interested in discovering superior products or services, but they need to see how these can help them accomplish their own objectives. As an example, I once met with an engineer, who contacted me to learn how to sell to large companies. He had developed a revolutionary product with many commercial applications.

He managed to secure important contracts with American electricity providers and was enquiring how to connect with engineers from the public hydro electricity provider located in the city where I lived. Due to his technical expertise, the engineer was wondering how to introduce the product to the engineering team. Instead, my recommendation was to focus on procurement. This could be done by presenting a business case with an explanation of how his technology had been allowing significant savings for similar customers. Since no demand existed for this revolutionary product, it was not possible simply to wait for public tenders. I also recommended the meeting invitation be extended to the engineering team through procurement in order to obtain better feedback and generate higher interest.

Process Optimization

Buyers are used to dealing with suppliers, internal clients, and following and establishing processes. For this reason, buyers are in a good position to make recommendations to fix operational issues. Optimizing how a company is working is not solely linked to supplier performance management, but should be done when opportunities arise.

By helping the business become more efficient, buyers are allowed to source better and add value for their customers. For example, if getting requirements to allow an RFP process is problematic, buyers can develop a scope of work template (a document outlining what information has to be provided by budget holders).

Another example could be that a buyer sees that budget holders are struggling to update their customers' address book. In this instance, procurement could ask its main parcel carrier for possible suggestions and introduce free software provided by the parcel company, software that is crying out to be used.

Some buyers may think it is not their business to help their internal customers beyond sourcing, but it definitely helps to be perceived as business partners. What this means for suppliers is that buyers should appreciate suggestions that can facilitate the purchaser's internal customers' work. Ultimately, this helps procurement improve sourcing coverage (the % of purchases managed or influenced by procurement) as procurement is seen as a proactive department.

SUPPORTING THE SCOPE OF WORK DESCRIPTION

When sourcing direct material (manufacturing goods), requirements usually come from technical specialists, such as engineers.

The dynamic is quite different when sourcing services (indirect procurement), because receiving thorough requirements is generally less frequent. This makes it harder for procurement to get involved in sourcing indirect categories if they don't proactively participate in outlining requirements.

It is quite normal for budget holders to find it difficult to provide requirements when requesting indirect categories; indirect suppliers are needed to provide expertise that the customer usually does not possess.

No matter the perceived challenge, sourcing indirect categories can be done for budget holders' benefits. While your requirements may not be as precise as those outlines by an engineer, if you describe the desired outcome this leaves the freedom for innovation to suppliers.

Buyers are in a good position to support the scope of work definition because they are used to communicating requirements to suppliers, have likely experienced similar sourcing projects, know what the market has to offer, and can even make their own suggestions.

In fact, budget holders from marketing, the hardest category to influence from a purchaser's standpoint, expect purchasers to support the process. As stated in a ANA survey on Procurement/Marketing Relationship from 2014 [6], RFI/RFP facilitation was listed as the top benefit that marketing procurement can bring to marketing.

To better understand and connect with budget holders (indirect), buyers should also seek involvement in service delivery. For example, one of the services that I was in charge of was acquiring event management services. To improve my knowledge in this area, I asked key stakeholders to invite me to their events, and I volunteered to handle the kids' Christmas party in which I was Santa Claus. Being in charge of delivering an event myself, I realized that my focus was more on delivery than on sourcing. The experience of handling an event allowed me to better understand the dynamic and the challenges that my clients face.

When you get to work more closely with suppliers, you come to realize that the traditional confrontational approach of procurement and the focus on price, is not going to get you very far. You also come to understand the advantages of working with long-term suppliers. Indeed, we have seen that procurement only influences 50% of marketing spending, demonstrating they often have the wrong agenda. According to a KPMG study from 2011[7] , procurement generally influenced less than 60% of spending across both direct and indirect categories. The following quotation from one of the book's reviewers describes the situation that is often seen:

"I often experienced a type of relationship that could qualify as confrontational. Each trying to seek their own benefits, with purchasers often taking a more aggressive approach during negotiation then the stakeholders, who are seeking a solution to their problem".[8]

The reason I highlight this quotation is to show that buyers need to evolve if they want to be accepted and expand their influence to 100% of addressable spending. As a buyer, if you are not even invited to the negotiation table, how can you have influence? One reader of my book – a purchaser - commented that it had the potential to help our counterparts in negotiation. I have also been told gently that I was a traitor. What buyers reading this book will hopefully realize is that I am sharing ways of working to cover all addressable spending and achieve much bigger impacts.

We will see later that it is possible to achieve huge savings by partnering and leveraging suppliers' expertise.

HANDLING COMMERCIAL DISCUSSIONS

Handling commercial discussions for large contracts requires experience and knowledge that budget holders are not likely to possess. Budget holders' contribution is essential, but their focus is more on delivery than on the commercial aspects. Additionally, many budget holders are not comfortable negotiating and prefer to leave this portion to procurement.

The reality is that purchasers are not always driving sourcing initiatives, but as I mentioned, this trend is gradually changing. It is not possible to provide exact statistics on spending, sourced or influenced by procurement versus internal clients (budget holders), as statistics differ based on industry, country, and categories. As a recap, a KPMG study from 2011 reported that procurement generally influenced less than 60% of spending across both direct and indirect categories.[9] Another report by CAPS from 2012 [10] revealed that the percentage of spending, managed/controlled by supply management was 83%. In this report, the financial service sector had one of the lowest percentages of spending, managed/controlled by supply management, with 70%.

In my opinion, the fact that procurement is more or less involved in some industries does not necessarily mean that there is added sourcing complexity. It appears that when a function, other than procurement, accounts for most of the profits, it tends to be harder for procurement to lead sourcing decisions.

For example, in manufacturing direct material purchases have huge impact on profits. As a result, procurement involvement is seen as essential. On the other hand, in the financial service industry, finance has a stronger influence on profitability than procurement. At some point in time, every industry should realize that maximizing profits and reaching efficiency could be achieved by improved collaboration between all departments.

Commercial discussions are usually handled differently for indirect service acquisitions than they are for direct goods acquisitions. A main difference is the frequent involvement of budget holders in negotiations for indirect purchases.

In general, it is beneficial when budget holders participate in commercial discussions, because it improves buy-in and ensures the service meets expectations. Below is an example of a sourcing project involving different stakeholders. This example illustrates that involving many stakeholders in indirect sourcing projects can result in information leakage.

PROCUREMENT AND INTERNAL STAKEHOLDERS ATTENDING SUPPLIERS' PRESENTATIONS

During a supplier's presentation to acquire a new service, a supplier became aware that we were interested in his proposal, but the end result played out differently than expected. While explaining the proposal, it was clear through non-verbal communication that the selection committee was satisfied with the offer.

However, the sourcing team did not receive the RFP responses well in advance of the presentation, thus the selection committee did not have the opportunity to analyze, in detail, the various proposals. As a result, the selection committee felt that they had a good proposal on the table when it was not the case.

Following the presentations, procurement noticed that another supplier had included a significant budget for gifts that the preferred potential supplier did not. Subsequently, procurement asked all suppliers to make slight design changes and present a final quotation. The lowest cost supplier came back with a lower price, and the preferred over-confident supplier had increased his price. When procurement called the "confident supplier" to inform him of the negative decision, the supplier was in a state of shock, because he thought that he had won the contract.

In this example, it is clear that information was miscommunicated. Unfortunately, the story did not end there. The supplier was very upset and expressed a lot of anger. The supplier mentioned, amongst other things, that a great deal of effort was invested in the RFP. The reason I am sharing the end result is to illustrate how expressing discontent is a big no-no. Buyers will never call back a rude supplier who has lost a contract, unless there are no other options.

Having the right attitude, even when losing a tender process will increase a supplier's chances of future bidding opportunities, as well as give them the opportunity to receive valuable feedback. Suppliers should remember that increasing prices following slight changes could also leave a bad impression; modifications do not necessarily need to mean higher costs.

More information regarding the advantages and inconvenient of the presence of budget holders in indirect commercial negotiations can be found in appendix 1 on page 94.

DISCLOSING BUDGETS DURING COMMERCIAL DISCUSSIONS

When sales professionals attempt to evaluate business potential they may enquire on business volume. This is usually not a problem, because it does not give indication of what the customer is paying or willing to pay. On the other hand, providing a budget for a customized service is likely to give an indication of how much the customer is willing to pay and should be avoided. This topic is important to cover, because there are more stakeholders involved when negotiating indirect related contracts.

Should Suppliers Ask Their Potential Customers For Budgets?

If the question is to understand business potential from a high-level perspective, then it is a question that can be asked. If the question is to figure out how much can be charged, then I believe it will leave a bad impression.

For example, if a wood floor installer asks you how much is budgeted to cover the floors in your home, the answer would probably be that you would like to be informed of the different options. At the back of your mind, you know that the vendor is trying to maximize his profits. This is no different when selling to large organizations.

Although providing budgets may seem strange to many and is not good practice, budgets are sometimes provided. Usually, when budgets are provided, it is done to speed-up acquisition. A good response to give to a supplier who is asking for a budget, is that it is his job to tell you how much something should cost. When faced with this question, buyers should ask what additional information should be provided to receive a quotation. If a supplier is proactive, there won't necessarily be a need to know a budget; instead, the supplier will be asking relevant questions to encourage the customer to define what is required and make suggestions. This approach is more conducive to gaining trust.

More details on the inconvenient and advantages of providing budget are available in appendix 2 on page 96.

Ensure Ethical Behaviors

It is a well-known fact that purchasers are in a sensitive situation, because they can impact business decisions. For this reason, there is a great emphasis on rules and ethical behaviour for procurement to follow. Ideally, other functions should also follow similar rules when engaging with suppliers, as they can sometimes have even greater influence than procurement.

Documenting the Acquisition Process and Sourcing Decisions

Medium and large size companies usually have a sourcing process to follow and have to document tender processes to support important purchasing decisions (over the sourcing limit). By doing so, buyers can gain and perpetuate knowledge from sourcing initiatives. Internal auditors, or sometimes internal stakeholders, may need to review these documents. Documenting the acquisition process is a way for purchasers to protect themselves and demonstrate transparency.

Supplier Performance Management (SPM)

As buyers and customers, we feel that it is up to suppliers to meet our expectations. For example, if an order is late, the initial reaction is to ask the "faulty" supplier for an action plan. In reality, issues can also arise from the customers' side. No matter where issues originate, it is best not to assume that customers will bear responsibility.

Formal SPM plans are mainly enacted for strategic suppliers, and performance is evaluated through KPIs (Key Performance Indicators) with the expectation of meeting an agreed service level (Service Level Agreement). In real life, the process may not be as strict and bullet proof as it appears, as measuring performance and satisfaction towards an indirect supplier involves many variables.

These variables are sometimes difficult to establish and track and can be subjective.

For less strategic suppliers or when a formal performance plan is not in place, there is still an ongoing evaluation that is occurring as clients are constantly monitoring smooth delivery of their products and/or services. Making this process more formal has advantages as it increases the odds for fair treatment and offers an opportunity for procurement to get to know the supplier and possibly recommend that supplier to other internal clients. The reason I mentioned "fair treatment" is simply because documenting and tracking performance can put things in perspective when issues occur.

Buyers are intermediaries in the relationships between internal clients and suppliers. As such, they are in a privileged position to lead SPM reviews and should definitely be contacted by suppliers to implement this process. Procurement should generally be supportive, because it is their mission to make their customers' lives easier and to better understand their purchasing habits.

Example of The Benefit of This Process:

Here is an example where setting monthly meetings to discuss performance issues and establish action plans have saved a troubled relationship.

In this example, a former supplier was eventually identified as a "bad supplier" and was replaced by a "good supplier" introduced by procurement. Two years after introducing the new supplier, key employees from both the supplier and our company left.

Those departures created a lack of continuity and eventually lead to total dissatisfaction with the supplier.

Compared to the first supplier who was replaced, the second one had strongly recommended frequent performance evaluation meetings, which never materialized. When the business relationship became critical, the second supplier mentioned the previous failed attempts at establishing evaluation meetings. As I could only agree that many attempts to track and review performance had been made, I was more inclined to give it a try. This was the right time to obtain collaboration from the budget holder due to an important upcoming web related project that had to be executed flawlessly.

At that point, I did not necessarily believe that the relationship would get better, as stakeholders and even procurement were extremely dissatisfied due to a one-sided version of the story. By holding monthly meetings, the issues were resolved, and we came out with stronger processes, faster lead-time, and improved satisfaction. Had we had not invested the time to resolve the issues, we would have had to switch again and no doubt face the same problems two years down the road. Acting as a middleman in the relationship, I was able to quickly identify the areas of opportunity on both sides. This changed the dynamic and once accusations were no longer being levied, we were able to work on finding solutions.

The enhanced business process was so successful that the supplier decided to implement similar enhanced processes with other customers. During this collaborative exercise, the suppliers had the opportunity to leverage a budget holder's strong expertise in project management, in addition to investing their own efforts.

MANAGING RISKS

Mitigating risk is an important procurement role, especially with direct procurement, as missing a single bolt or having a defective component could have a huge financial impact. Reputational risks and data protection issues are also daily considerations for buyers.

Buyers have to minimize supply and quality risks by various means, such as selecting the most reliable suppliers, ensuring that appropriate BCP's (business continuity plans) are in place, establishing contingency plans, drafting appropriate commercial agreements, and leading or supporting contractual agreements.

Late deliveries and quality issues are constant threats to a buyer's peace of mind (especially in manufacturing). Proactive suppliers can implement processes to minimize the occurrence of problems. Advertising risk mitigation measures to procurement and budget holders is a great way for entrepreneurs or sales representatives to put more focus on reliability than cost.

For example, there are many importers that deal with lower-cost countries. From my experience, I have found that most suppliers communicate having good relationships with their manufacturers. However, the reality is that the level of risk in working with importers varies greatly from one supplier to another.

For importers, it is important to educate your customers on the risks and actions that are in place to protect them. If an importer has a great model and buyers know about it, they are more likely to ask relevant questions to competitors and to better appreciate where a good importer stands compared with others.

Examples of rational criteria that should influence purchasing decisions with an importer:

- No upfront payment is necessary, because the importer is not only confident, but willing to assume risks

- Penalties in case of late deliveries or quality issues

- Adequate insurance coverage

- Accountability for product defects and returns

- Ability to ensure compliance with local regulations

- Initiatives to reduce environmental footprint

- Focus on minimizing reputational issues by auditing third party suppliers and their subcontractors

- Actions to maintain good relationships with government regulators

- Proactivity in performing due diligence when importing new products. For example, developing quality tests when none exist or are not mandatory

- Hiring a foreign worker (s) at the importer's office to ease communications

- Financial strength and stability so that potential issues can be covered by profits, and the importer has higher leverage toward its manufacturers

- Proper suggested Incoterms protecting buyers

From my observations, very few suppliers spend adequate time explaining how they manage risks for their customers. Going back to the importer example, when importing large quantities, issues on a single order can produce a loss. While experienced buyers may be aware of the importance of managing risks, one can never assume what buyers and budget holders actually know. This expertise varies, according to each organisation and individual.

Risks can also take the form of unexpected costs. For example, there may be penalties when projects are cancelled or business volume is not reached. From my experience, suppliers generally do not establish prices for samples, because they expect to cover these costs through an order that ultimately may get cancelled. To cover for this risk, it is recommended that suppliers establish sample costs at the outset of new projects; they can add a note that the sample will be free of charge if the project or order is executed.

By laying out cancellation or sample costs in advance, suppliers are not only receiving financial protection, but they are also protecting their reputation. Agreeing in advance on these costs forces stakeholders to confirm that the order is likely to happen. If the order is cancelled, then the customer will not feel that the supplier is taking advantage of them, because prices were known in advance.

SAVINGS

I know that many suppliers feel frustrated when they are faced with aggressive buyers, who seem to only care about the cost. There is a feeling that all that is done to please customers is not taken into consideration, especially when buyers are not the ones experiencing service delivery.

Although most procurement professionals do not define themselves as being cost cutters, there seems to be a consensus that it is procurement's main mission to control expenditure. To support this, an internal survey was conducted with 457 procurement executives in 16 countries by spending management solution provider, Ivalua. The survey revealed that 75% of respondents claimed that cost reduction is the line of businesses that procurement can affect most.[11] In a 2013 survey conducted with 113 marketing procurement professionals by ANA (Association of National Advertising), 94% of respondents claimed that cost reduction was the most important metric measuring the success of marketing procurement.[12]

SAVING CALCULATIONS

By understanding how savings are calculated, entrepreneurs and sales representative will gain a better understanding of this important metric for buyers.

It is important to know that saving definitions can vary from one organization to the next. For example, a company may consider a saving claimed by a buyer, only if a budget gets reduced.

Another company may accept a saving, even though there is no budget reduction, since lower costs allow for an increase in volume. The following example illustrates two scenarios. In the first one, a budget is reduced as a result of a price negotiation. In the second one, the budget is maintained although price was negotiated.

1) Reduced budget as a result of price negotiations:

The following example (purchase of promotional billboards) illustrates the saving impact when a company does not maintain its budget as a result of lower costs.

In this example, the unit price is negotiated from $100 per board per week to $40 and the annual budget is reduced from $100,000 to $40,000. This negotiation results in an indirect savings of $60,000.

Initial budget	Initial unit price	Negotiated unit price	Price difference	No. Billboards	Revised budget	Indirect Savings
$100,000	$100	$40	$60	1,000	$40,000	$60,000

Figure 5

2) Similar budget with a reduction in unit price and increased volume:

In this example, the unit price is also negotiated at $40 but the budget remains the same. This negotiation results in an indirect savings of $150,000.

Initial budget	Initial unit price	Negotiated unit price	Price difference	No. Billboards	Same budget	Indirect Savings
$100,000	$100	$40	$60	2,500	$100,000	$150,000

Figure 6

In the second example, the budget holder is eager to maintain investment, as its main objective is to increase visibility.

In my opinion, buyers prefer the second scenario, because savings are an important part of their job; maintaining budgets can result in bigger savings for buyers (when it is accepted by finance as a saving). When new finance managers review this type of saving, they usually ask for an explanation as to why there were savings, despite having no impact on the budget.

The response lies with an increase in visibility, which in theory, should lead to an increase in sales (for marketing related products or services). Since the objective of all companies is to make a profit, indirect savings, as per this example, are important.

Reducing budgets is a good strategy that companies can use to motivate budget holders to increase collaboration with procurement, but this should be a gradual process, not directly linked to specific sourcing initiatives. Not doing so may make it harder for procurement to get involved.

It is a fact that indirect savings are not hitting the bottom line as much as direct savings. For example, if the price of a manufacturing component is reduced, the company will not necessarily need more components. Thus, the impact on the bottom line is more likely than an indirect saving.

In both scenarios, the savings was calculated by comparing an initial price to a negotiated price. When historical prices exist, calculating savings is generally straightforward.

For example, if a consultant was paid $100 an hour, and the negotiated rate is now $90, then buyers can claim a 10$ saving per hour. In order for the saving calculation to be accepted, buyers need to compare similar products or services while taking volume into consideration.

Savings are usually calculated for a one-year period. Following that period, buyers have to reduce rates further in order to continue claiming savings. Buyers may not be allowed to claim savings if the price reduction is only a matter of increased volume.

To avoid situations where buyers would have a hard time explaining their savings rationale, cautious buyers should develop the habit of asking in advance for volume discounts or price brackets for different volumes. Suppliers can also be proactive and provide the information as a standard business practice.

As you can well appreciate, it is quite challenging for buyers to continually meet their saving objectives, as suppliers will not gratuitously offer rate reductions every year. As an employee, I must admit that I would not embrace a salary decrease every year either.

Achieving savings on newly acquired products or services is harder to accomplish, as there are no historical prices. In this case, savings are generally calculated by comparing the RFP rates against the negotiated rates. When suppliers have already submitted their most competitive rates, negotiating further is not easy.

OTHER WAYS TO OBTAIN OR GENERATE SAVINGS

Sharing discounts from third party suppliers

In addition to negotiating better rates, procurement can also obtain savings from suppliers that negotiate on their behalf.

Reporting savings made on third party suppliers is a good strategy that can save customers money and help to solidify relationships. For example, one of our suppliers had to buy material for some activities, and I asked them to track every saving that was made. Doing so helped procurement reach their saving objectives, while promoting a true partnership between the two parties.

When suppliers contribute to saving objectives, buyers are more accommodating when demands for reasonable price increases are presented. The key is to report savings to procurement so that it can be taken into consideration. This can be done on an annual or bi-annual basis by sharing detailed supporting documents, such as invoices. It can be time consuming, but the benefits are manifold.

Change of Methods

Another way to obtain savings is to purchase services or products that are more efficient than previous one.

For example, let's assume that your company's customer orders were captured through customer representatives. A new technology now allows customers to input their orders online. Since both methods achieve the same objective (taking orders), the savings would be based on a cost comparison between the two methodologies.

For this saving to be recognized, the initiative should be taken by procurement. Suppliers are, therefore, advised to contact procurement when they think they have innovative ways of fulfilling business objectives.

As a second example, a quotation was once requested on a print project.

The mandate was to print on a white surface with a magnet underneath. As the preferred supplier was encouraged to share insights on ways to reduce costs, the printer instead suggested printing on removable stickers. This advice resulted in significant savings while meeting the objective.

TRADITIONAL WAY TO SUPPORT CUSTOMERS' SAVING OBJECTIVES

As illustrated in the previous examples, innovative solutions can lead to important savings. However, pure cost reductions are, and probably will remain, strategies sought after by most procurement professionals.

The good news is that offering lower rates is not always negative. The following examples explain traditional saving suggestions that can be mutually beneficial.

Offering Discounts in Exchange for Longer-Term Commitments

When securing new contracts, entrepreneurs/sales representatives could suggest incentives in exchange for extending contract terms. There is a tendency for suppliers to respond to what their customers ask, but nothing forbids them from making suggestions.

This is clearly an advantage, because it secures business for a longer period and reduces the cost and efforts associated with acquiring new business. Although this is a very simplistic recommendation, I have rarely been offered this opportunity without having to ask for it.

This recommendation has a better chance of being accepted by buyers and budget holders when prices for specific products or services tend to remain stable or increase over time.

This suggestion may be less appealing when prices follow a downward trend, as with computers and telecoms in certain countries. No matter the situation, it does not cost much to suggest.

Offering Volume Discounts in Exchange for Similar and/or Greater Budgets

This strategy is especially relevant if you are in an industry where spending is reduced in a downward economy (e.g. advertising during recessions). Budget holders may see a benefit to maintaining their existing budget by promoting the added value of a discount. Procurement is also likely to support the initiative, as it would help toward their saving objectives. When budgets are split between several suppliers, offering volume discounts may result in more business for proactive suppliers.

Offering a Discount Versus Free Products in Exchange for Maintaining Investment

An alternative to offering lower rates/discounts or rebates is to offer free products in exchange for maintaining investment. In the following example, we will see that offering free products is more beneficial than lowering costs.

Example with Advertising Billboards

In this example, the historical price from the previous year was $100 per billboard and the customer purchased it for $100,000. The supplier's unit cost is $70 with a gross margin of 30%.

Supplier Unit Cost	Profit	Price	Quantity	Total Price for Customer	Procurement Indirect Savings	Supplier Profit	Gross Margin
$70	$30	$100	1 000	$100 000	0	$30 000	30,0%

Figure 7

1) Offering a discount: a supplier offers a 5% discount on the selling price. The selling price is lowered from $100 to $95 and the supplier gross margin is reduced to 26,3%.

Supplier Unit Cost	Profit	Price	Quantity	Total Price for Customer	Procurement Indirect Savings	Supplier Profit	Gross Margin
$70	$25	$95	1 000	$95 000	$5 000	$25 000	26,3%

Figure 8

2) Offering free products for maintaining investment: the supplier offers 5% in free products if the customer maintains equal investment. In this example, the unit price is reduced from $100 to 95,24$, the customer has 50 additional billboards and the supplier's gross margin is 26,5%

Supplier Unit Cost	Profit	Price	Quantity	Total Price for Customer	Procurement Indirect Savings	Supplier Profit	Gross Margin
$70	$25,24	$95,24	1 050	$100 000	$5 000	$26 500	26,5%

Figure 9

Seeing that there is a margin on what is being sold, offering free products in exchange for a similar level of investment is a better financial option for suppliers than simply reducing prices through a discount. In the second scenario, the supplier earns an additional $1500 in profit. In both scenarios, procurement should be able to claim a $5,000 saving.

Establishing Prices According to Volume

Most purchasers will generally provide best forecast and expect to pay a rate accordingly. This is definitely the most comfortable position, because it represents a "soft" commitment. For sales professionals, this may not represent the best option, as some buyers (not a majority in my experience) may exaggerate on volume to obtain better prices.

For example, I have met with a pretty aggressive buyer, who told me that she negotiated with hotels by stating higher volumes than expected to obtain lower rates. When the time for contract renewal came, one of the hotels complained that they had been far from receiving the expected volume. The answer to the hotel representative was that volume was low because of high prices.

A recommendation to avoid granting discounts not aligned with business volume is to recommend a discount plan, where the calculation and the remittance are provided at the end of a specific term. This strategy can also provide an incentive to purchasers to ensure employees respect the agreement to maximize procurement savings.

Not all purchases are subject to a tender process. For example, purchases under a sourcing limit can be awarded to existing prequalified suppliers without a formal quotation process. Offering volume discounts with achievable volume targets provides an incentive to direct investment.

What I have experienced is that most companies usually agree to provide volume discounts when being asked, but they hope that buyers will forget about them. Instead, the recommended strategy is to leverage such agreement.

When a company offers a discount, it is important that it is advertised properly. For example, I recommend making discounts visible on all quotes and invoices. This extra visibility helps to reinforce the partnership perception and increase the odds of securing orders, especially when competitors are not offering discounts. When new volume threshold brackets are about to be reached, customers should receive a call, informing them of the opportunity.

When a credit note is issued at the end of the year, it represents a good opportunity to meet with buyers and/or budget holders and ask for feedback. All of this attention helps solidify business relationships. When not advertised, volume discounts can become wasted money.

If you are selling products or services where prices vary a lot between orders and are hard to assess by customers, then a discount may not mean much in reality. No matter, it can make a difference to the partnership perception.

I will share an example where a discount could have saved the day for a supplier. This example also illustrates how attitude can impact business decisions.

Example: Issue with a print project

I had been confronted by a situation where a supplier did not perform a printing job according to our "standards." After enquiring, I concluded that it was not the supplier's fault, but the problem originated from an approval process issue. No matter the facts, the budget holder felt that the supplier should have known that we expected more and wanted them to redo a print job at his own expense.

The supplier really felt that nothing had been done wrong and did not want to indemnify the customer. I suggested that we simply used a portion of the annual credit note to cover the loss. The supplier thanked me, but refused as a matter of principle. The internal client decided to get rid of the print job, so it would not affect his brand image. There was no budget left!

Although unfair, the decision not to accept my offer significantly impacted future orders, as the budget holder felt that the supplier did not value the privileged relationship. In this situation, procurement was not in a position to influence future spending, because most print purchases were under the souring limit and were managed by our agency that selects print suppliers. As the agency cannot risk upsetting its client, they had to take that into consideration.

Another supplier told me a similar story, where a supposed defect was found on one if his products. Following a complaint, that supplier decided to test all products and did not find any issue. Since the product was no longer required once testing was completed, he had been asked to absorb the loss. The supplier told me that he accepted, because it was more beneficial to do so. The moral of the story is that when an important client complains, it may be wiser to accept a loss. The annual rebate could serve to cover these unpleasant issues that sometimes arise (when procurement accepts).

Possible confusion when calculating an Annual Credit

When a company offers an annual credit based on volume, it is recommended to explain how the credit will be calculated as it can be confusing.

In this example, let's assume that a customer had purchased for a total of $250,000 over a one-year period.

Scenario 1:

If a credit is calculated on overall business volume as per the following discount table below, a 6% discount on a $250,000 annual expenditure would represent a $15,000 credit (6% X $250,000). This calculation is easy to understand and calculate.

Discount/ Credit	Annual Volume	Indirect Savings
2.00%	$0 to $100,000	
4.00%	$100,001 to $200,000	
6.00%	$200,001 to $300,000	$15,000

Figure 10

Scenario 2:

The other way to calculate a credit is to apply the appropriate percentage discount at each bracket. Under the following scenario, a $250,000 annual expenditure represents a $9,000 discount (2% X $100,000, + 4% X $100,000, + 6% X $50,000).

Discount/ Credit	Annual Volume	Indirect Savings
2.00%	$0 to $100,000	$2,000
4.00%	$100,001 to $200,000	$4,000
6.00%	$200,001 to $300,000	$3,000

Total: $9,000

Figure 11

As we can appreciate, scenario 2 is in fact equivalent to a 3.6% discount under the first scenario. For simplicity's sake, I prefer the first calculation because it is less confusing for everyone.

I don't believe that offering an annual credit based on volume will influence all purchasing decisions, but depending on the situation, it can help secure additional business. Granted credits should generally have more impact during the first year, as buyers can usually claim savings during a one-year period only.

For this reason, incrementing annual rebates on a second year, instead of giving a higher rebate on the first year, can be beneficial. This extended period offers the opportunity to increase interactions with procurement and provides an extra incentive for purchasers to track or intervene in case of non-compliance.

Removing a discount program after one year can prove to be problematic, especially for direct purchases where cost for each component is usually tracked pretty closely. From my experience, indirect costs are not tracked as much as direct costs. This is due to the nature of services and the challenges of tracking these costs.

Concluding On Buyers' Roles

As you have seen, procurement handles different tasks and is not only working toward reducing costs. Knowing what procurement does offers different opportunities to interact with them.

Some areas of purchasing (indirect categories) are still relatively new to procurement, but their influence is increasing. Learning how to better interact with buyers can certainly open new bidding opportunities. A main reason for that is that budget holders generally prefer to remain with existing service providers. As a result, purchasers can become allies that can introduce new ideas and superior suppliers to budget holders.

CHAPTER 2 TAKEAWAYS

- Corporations hire buyers not only to save on costs but to perform other tasks such as: leading supplier performance management, optimizing processes, overseeing and documenting acquisition processes, ensuring that suppliers are treated fairly, promoting innovation, helping stakeholders better express their needs (especially with services), managing risks, screening and recommending suppliers, acting as a main point of contact for existing and new suppliers, enforcing ethical behaviours and handling commercial discussions.

- It is a fact that buyers need to report savings. Savings can be achieved by working with a lower cost supplier or negotiating with current suppliers. To avoid reducing their bottom line, suppliers can share savings from third party suppliers and/or leverage their expertise and make innovative recommendations that can lead to efficiency savings. Innovative ways of supplying goods and services can produce more savings for buyers than simply asking for rate reductions.

- Proactive suppliers generally do not need budgets; they are able to guide their customers in defining their requirements.

CHAPTER 3: CHALLENGES OF ACQUIRING NEW CUSTOMERS

This chapter explains the challenges that sales professionals face when looking for new customers and when purchasers are dealing with new suppliers. This knowledge will allow all stakeholders (buyers, entrepreneurs, sales representatives, budget holders, and suppliers) to understand the strategies aimed at maximizing sourcing/selling outcomes.

Everyone has heard that you can learn to be good at sales. If you acquire the proper sales techniques, you will likely increase results, close deals, and even sell ice to an Eskimo. All of the above may be true, but becoming and remaining a supplier for a private company requires more than behavioural knowledge and can be difficult.

There is no magic formula to acquiring new customers as there are many obstacles. Let's look at some of these challenges in order to better understand the recommended strategies.

In this chapter, we will look at the main challenges facing companies who wish to acquire new customers. Sales professionals that deal with large multinationals may face different acquisition contexts. For example, they may interact directly with the company's headquarters, with only one or many affiliates and even with third parties managing procurement activities.

PERSONAL RELATIONSHIPS

The human element is important, especially when dealing with service providers. Some suppliers may even be likened to employees, having been around for many years. This makes it difficult to get a foot in the door.

CURRENT SUPPLIERS' KNOWLEDGE

Imagine a department where employees rotate positions every two years. In this scenario, suppliers are typically more knowledgeable than their customers and are therefore, harder to replace.

As most customers have developed brand preferences, the same is true for internal stakeholders. If they like their service providers, they won't feel the need for change. It is much easier and less disruptive to ask current suppliers to improve on specific criteria, such as price. For this reason, better commercial offers and skilled sales representatives or entrepreneurs are sometimes not enough to trigger change.

SUPPLIER RATIONALIZATION

As a day-to-day customer, you probably prefer to shop in bigger stores, rather than small shops. The same is true for corporations; they find it more efficient to lower their suppliers' base. Most large companies have KPIs (Key Performance Indicators) aimed at reducing suppliers.

STRATEGIC SUPPLIERS

Although this book provides insight on how to acquire new customers, there are strategic suppliers that cannot be easily replaced given their criticality and the complexities of their operations. For example, when companies outsource some of their core activities, the efforts required to get a strong partnership can represent a significant deterrent from considering other potential partners. In this case, it may be more efficient to work on continuous improvement initiatives, rather than seeking other partners through market solicitations. Some examples of strategic suppliers are marketing agencies, third party logistic providers, and critical direct material suppliers. Due to this reality, acquiring new customers can be a real challenge for strategic suppliers.

ADMINISTRATIVE

Dealing with a new supplier can generate many administrative tasks, such as: setting up a vendor in an IT system, validating references, enquiring about the company's credit history, signing a NDA (non-disclosure agreement), creating a purchase order, drafting a contract, and paying a supplier. In other words, all of these require time and money.

CONFIDENTIALITY

The more suppliers you deal with, confidentiality becomes harder to protect. For IT-related services, large corporations are likely to conduct IT security audits to ensure data protection.

This can make it harder for smaller suppliers with fewer resources to comply with hard to meet requirements.

RECENT RFP PROCESS

Sales professionals prospecting new customers may be reaching a company that has just gone through a lengthy sourcing process. The next opportunity may only present itself in a few years.

TRANSITION COSTS

Although a supplier may offer the best price, there are probably transition costs to consider. As an example, switching software providers with links to other systems can be costly. Sometimes, these transition costs can be discovered during a sourcing process and influence decisions.

Sourcing Limit

Strategic buyers are usually not involved in every transaction. They generally work with sourcing limits that can range from $500 to $100,000 plus. The reason is simple: companies cannot afford to hire hundreds of buyers. Buyers can achieve the best return on investment when they focus on high-cost acquisitions. Unfortunately, some companies have too much work for their procurement department and don't realize that employees should focus limited resources where it counts.

For entrepreneurs or sales representatives, it means that if you are selling services or products that represent an expense that is under a sourcing limit, chances are that it won't be a priority to run quotations. This is especially the case when the service is already good and the price deemed competitive.

On the other hand, if what you are selling represents an investment over the sourcing limit, there is an increased chance that a buyer will need to get involved in the acquisition. When tender processes are required, it usually opens up bidding opportunities for new suppliers.

Contracts and Internal Requirements

Depending on the products or services that need to be purchased, companies can sign exclusivity contracts for specific periods of time. In addition, lengthy internal contractual processes can outweigh the benefits of dealing with a superior supplier.

Decision Makers

Since purchasers are not always driving sourcing initiatives, especially with indirect procurement (services), entrepreneurs and sales representatives may wonder whom to contact when they wish to sell to private companies.

Procurement/supply chain involvement varies greatly between industries, countries, and companies.

Since some organizations are not likely to tolerate or appreciate suppliers bypassing procurement, it is always recommended to reach out to procurement first when enquiring about how to potentially sell to new corporate customers.

Payment Terms

Large companies usually pay their supplier with extended payment terms that can range from 30 days to 180 days. This can cause cash flow issues for smaller suppliers. Enquiring about early payment discount can be worthwhile.

Global Procurement Influence

There is a trend for multinationals to centralize procurement. By doing so, economies of scale are expected, and procurement expertise can be leveraged. This reality can make it more complex to interact with global purchasers that are located miles away and influence them.

Since global purchasers are more likely to be dealing with multiple countries and suppliers, they can't spend much time developing relationships with many suppliers. To complicate matters, there are no standard procurement models. Global purchasers can rely on their local procurement teams or interact directly with suppliers. The relationship usually depends on the product or service being sourced and the procurement maturity level or preference. There is no perfect model.

When global purchasers are looking to secure global deals, they obviously prefer dealing with global suppliers that can centralize communication to a main contact. This means that global suppliers without a centralized structure could benefit from centralizing communications to a main point of contact. This would accommodate customers who wish to streamline communications.

To better understand the different purchasing contexts faced when dealing with multinationals, you will find below more explanations on global versus local purchasers.

Dealing With Global Versus Local Purchasers

You will find below some differences between dealing with a local purchaser (Affiliate Company (ies) or with a global purchaser who negotiates deals on behalf of many affiliates.

Differences

	Global Purchasers	Local Purchasers (Affiliates)
Relationship with suppliers	More distant	Closer
Relationship with budget holders (Indirect purchases)	More distant	Closer
Focus	Economies of scale/savings	Budget holders' satisfaction and savings
Preferred supplier's business models	1 point of contact covering multiple countries	Maximum benefit out of every supplier, consolidating only when justified

Figure 12

As we saw, dealing with global purchasers offers a different context. The following strategies can help increase the odds of securing deals with global purchasers.

Connecting Better With Global Purchasers

- As much as possible, interactions with global purchasers should be made in person and by phone, rather than solely answering e-mails. This will help build a relationship and may help gain valuable information.

- It is important to demonstrate to the global purchasers that you possess a good understanding of your customers' needs. This can influence the outcome, as global purchasers do not want their customers to face issues and have to deal with complaints.

- It may be necessary to help global buyers understand what they are buying (in the event that there is a lack of knowledge); not all purchasers were selected based on specific category expertise.

- Offer to consolidate spending and savings to support global purchasers. This may be appreciated in the event that the customer's purchasing systems do not provide consolidated spending reports (across affiliates).

- Establish and agree on a global agreement with preferential rates, rebates, special payment terms, price lists, etc. This agreement has to be short and simple, so that the global purchasers can easily forward to other affiliates.

- Be proactive; come up with ideas and solutions that will demonstrate to your customers that they are saving money, thanks to your recommendations. This will make you a preferred partner, and global purchasers will recommend buying from your company.

- If you offer a product for which no demand exists, share a price list; offer retroactive discounts in the event that certain volumes are reached and communicate savings progress. If there is no financial incentive that can be easily reported, global purchasers will probably not promote your products or services.

- Offer to build a private website for important customers to make products and services available to all affiliates through global transparent price lists. Capabilities such as order tracking, consulting purchasing history, and satisfaction survey results, are likely to be valued.

As we have seen, there are many challenges making it difficult to become a supplier. We have also started to review some strategies to interact better with global purchasers.

CHAPTER 3 TAKEAWAYS

- Due to numerous challenges, sometimes being the best company and sales representative does not guarantee sales. It is essential to exploit every opportunity to influence purchasing decisions.

- Due to the gradual introduction of purchasers in service acquisition, knowing who to contact certainly can be confusing when prospecting. The first point of contact should be the procurement department.

- The globalization efforts of multinationals to increase purchasing leverage influences how prospecting and selling is conducted.

- Human relations are important when dealing with global and local purchasers. Like local purchasers, global purchasers are not necessarily experts at sourcing specific products or services. This reality can offer an opportunity to engage. Before contacting a global purchaser of a multinational, it is best to get support from a local purchaser when relevant.

So far we have reviewed basic procurement terminologies, the challenges of acquiring/selling services, why corporations hire buyers and the challenges of becoming a supplier. Now that we understand better the acquisition context related with indirect procurement, we will review the strategic sourcing process and what can be done at each step to maximize outcomes.

Chapter 4: Maximizing Outcomes of Strategic Sourcing Processes

This chapter explains the main steps of a strategic sourcing process. The strategic sourcing process generally begins by identifying areas of interest for purchasers through a spending analysis. The phase that consists of analyzing sourcing opportunities, generally based on spending, will not be covered.

The likelihood that a complete sourcing process is performed is influenced by several variables including: sourcing policy, sourcing policy enforcement, amounts involved, criticality of the acquisitions, lead-time available to source, procurement maturity level, stakeholder availability and collaboration etc.

Following a strict procurement process that covers all phases is not necessary for all purchases. For example, acquisitions under a sourcing limit or repetitive purchases do not necessarily require you to follow each step for each order. When time is limited, skipping steps is often needed.

No matter how strict or flexible a company's procurement process is, understanding how purchasers, budget holders and suppliers collaborate is essential to improve knowledge of B2B for indirect purchases.

Strategic Sourcing Process covered

Figure 13

1) Needs Identification

Gaining Knowledge on Products and/or Services

The first thing a purchaser does when receiving a requisition (requirement to perform a sourcing activity) is to gather as much knowledge as possible about what has to be sourced.

Gaining knowledge at the outset of a sourcing process allows procurement to support budget holders in defining their requirements, suggest alternatives, and allow the development of sourcing strategies.

To gain further knowledge, buyers can rely on different sources of information.

Sources of Information available to purchasers

- Past RFPs or RFQs
- Invoices
- Other stakeholders who have acquired similar products and/or services
- Web searches
- External resources (procurement associations, consulting firms like Gartner and Forrester, other buyers, etc.)
- Meeting actual and potential suppliers
- Issue an RFI or informally obtain input

In addition to initial investigations, purchasers will need to obtain more details about what has to be sourced from budget holders. For both direct and indirect purchases, putting oneself in a supplier's shoes will provide the necessary mindset to properly document and eventually communicate requirements to suppliers.

For example, buyers and budget holders should be asking this question to themselves:

If I were a supplier receiving these requirements, would I have enough details to understand what to quote on, without having to ask additional questions?

By simply thinking this, it becomes easier to understand what additional information needs to be obtained and provided.

Learning how to best express needs can speed up the acquisition process, reduce issues, and as a result offer an opportunity to strengthen relationships between procurement and budget holders.

Identifying requirements is performed somehow differently for direct versus indirect purchases.

DEFINING REQUIREMENTS FOR DIRECT GOODS

For direct goods acquisitions (manufacturing), most needs are identified and communicated to procurement by function experts, such as engineers. When procurement receives requests (called requisitions), buyers usually have to ask basic questions to complement technical requirements such as:

- Required date

- Estimated annual volume

- Delivery locations

- Possibility of purchasing product substitutes

- Quality standards

When acquiring new components, procurement is likely to be involved in the development phase by working hand-in-hand with engineers. This collaboration ensures that the components are not imposed by engineers, but are sourced according to a competitive process.

Buyers can also be proactive by investigating alternative products or new technologies that may benefit the company.

For example, during a recession, a company that supplies the automotive industry with metal parts made of metal powder, instead of raw material (high volume), decided to expand its customer base in the medical industry. This supplier allowed procurement to shine, because the supplier was able to meet quality standards and supply metal parts at a much better price.

DEFINING REQUIREMENTS FOR INDIRECT GOODS & SERVICES

Requirements for indirect purchases can come from different functions, such as IT, finance, marketing, and HR. The requirements are usually less technical than for direct purchases. This is why indirect buyers are more likely to have some influence over budget holders when needs are defined. This also means suppliers are more likely to have the possibility of influencing what is being bought by engaging with buyers and budget holders.

When receiving an indirect purchasing request, buyers will usually have to ask additional questions to budget holders on topics like:

- Objectives

- Priorities

- Quantities

- Dates

- Budget

- Quality

- Roles and responsibilities

- Potential concerns

- Internal requirements from other departments (legal, IT, health and safety)

To illustrate how to communicate needs for an indirect purchase, I will provide two examples. In the first one, we will see that it is possible to obtain quotations without providing too much information in a range of different scenarios. In the second example, we will see that a proactive buyer could benefit from leveraging suppliers' expertise to better understand a service and improve budget holder's support when defining requirements.

Example 1: Trade Booth Acquisition:

Scenario 1: relying on an external marketing agency not specializing in trade booths

A budget holder asks its marketing agency to develop a trade booth concept (design for inspiration) and to prepare a brief to explain execution requirements.

This information is shared with procurement, which clarifies and improves the scope of work through discussions with budget holders and the agency. An RFP is then sent to a shortlist of suppliers.

Examples of basic requirements that procurement is likely to enquire about:

- Dimensions

- Dates

- Communication requirements (examples: projection, screens, audio, printed fabrics etc.)

- Quality attributes (examples: how long should the booth last, touch and feel etc.)

- Required warranties

- Support services (examples: set-up and dismantling, cleaning, animation, catering services, etc.)

- Warehousing and transportation requirements

- Budgets

Since a concept is provided in the first scenario, suppliers are likely to come up with quite similar proposals in terms of design. The concept constraint would ideally not limit suppliers' creativity, especially when suppliers are told they can suggest enhancements and propose options.

In this sourcing context, conducting an RFP is likely to result in:

- Increased bargaining power for procurement, as several suppliers can quote

- More options for the budget holder

Receiving more than one proposal allows the budget holder to select the best option. The mere possibility of choosing what is best constitutes a key incentive to obtain support from budget holders to participate in a sourcing process.

Scenario 2: Relying on Suppliers' Expertise

In this scenario, a budget holder provides execution guidelines and high-level look and feel expectations to procurement. Procurement helps clarify the scope of work and run an RFP.

In this scenario, the buyer would probably rent an existing booth, instead of acquiring a custom-built solution. Given limited design guidance, it is expected that very different propositions will be presented.

Scenario 3: Sole Sourcing With Limited Support From Procurement

In this example, a budget holder calls a long-term supplier. The budget holder and the supplier spend a month reviewing designs and finally agree on what is required through ongoing communications. Once issuing an order becomes urgent to meet a deadline, procurement receives a quotation from a budget holder and is told that a PO should be issued in the coming days in order to meet a deadline.

Different outcomes:

- The first scenario (relying on an external agency for design) should result in comparable designs with different prices (when no budget is provided). This scenario is likely to end up being expensive because a custom solution is needed.

- The second scenario (relying on suppliers' expertise) is likely to provide very different solutions with a wider range of prices. One of the cheapest solutions is likely to come up from this scenario because existing booths can probably be reused.

- The third scenario (sole source with limited procurement support) will not allow any price and design comparison. One of the perceived advantages is that the budget holder can start engaging without delay with a known supplier. To speed up the project, a budget is likely to be provided. The reality is that this process may take longer, as needs are usually not very detailed and much back and forth is required.

These scenarios indicate that there are various ways to engage with suppliers, and different outcomes are expected

Example 2: leveraging suppliers' expertise for a Retail Engagement Program

We will now review an example that illustrates how leveraging suppliers' expertise can be a good way to obtain more input to better support internal clients during the need definition phase.

In this example, a budget holder asks procurement to find a supplier to perform a retail engagement program. The requirement is to find a supplier who could visit 15,000 stores in a two-week period in order to collect information from store owners. The obligation to seek collaboration from procurement is dictated by a sourcing policy that states that projects over a certain amount should follow a sourcing process.

In this example, the budget holder was not able to produce a complete brief and procurement had to do some extra work to get more input from the internal client. The first thing that the buyer did was to simply imagine that he was a supplier having to quote on the project.

This allowed him to come up with precise questions that needed to be answered by the budget holder.

Additional basic information to enquire on:

- Objectives of the program

- Locations to be visited

- Actions that the visitors should perform in each store

- Dates

- Attributes of the staff needed

- Reporting needs

- Potential concerns

- Internal requirements from other departments

- Suppliers suggestions of who could perform the mandate (when procurement is not aware)

After receiving more input from the budget holder, the buyer was able to discuss the project with potential suppliers. In doing so, the buyer took the opportunity to ask further questions to learn about: the service, the cost drivers, ways to save on costs, best practices, variables needed to obtain a quotation etc.

Following the interactions with potential suppliers, the buyer assembled a list of 31 variables that needed further clarification from the budget holder. Below is presented a sample of these variables.

Additional Variables Obtained from Potential Suppliers

Program:

- Program length

- Time of year

- Period of day restrictions/requirements

Survey Details:

- Data collection requirements and reporting

- Number of products to enquire over

- Required Languages

Store Details:

- List of stores to visit

- Completion % required

- Number of visits per store

- Busy staff instructions

Optional Services:

- Printing of forms

- Translation of documents

- Long-distance calls

- Customer supports (telephone and/or emails)

- Customized website

The buyer has also learned elements to consider when evaluating suppliers' quality processes and gained knowledge of ways to save on costs. With this extra knowledge, the buyer is now in a much better position to clarify the project scope for an eventual RFP.

When budget holders meet with well-prepared buyers, the reaction is likely to be positive, especially if communicating requirements used to be a long exercise. When requirements are not communicated at once, it is impossible to run an RFP and there are increased chances for costs to exceed budgets and face many more issues.

This example illustrates how leveraging suppliers' expertise can be beneficial for all stakeholders. By defining requirements from the outset with procurement support, budget holders will save time, have the possibility to receive multiple quotations and thus have a greater variety of options to choose from.

On their side, suppliers will have the opportunity to engage with the buyer and/or budget holder, thus becoming closer to securing an order. In this example, the buyer is proactive and this enabled him to gradually build internal credibility and expertise.

Sometimes, in order to know what is required, a lot of consulting with a supplier is necessary. In such context, a tender process may appear to be less appropriate.

A good example would be a large corporate event six months down the road. Comparing proposals in this context requires adapting the evaluation methodology and making a decision without necessarily knowing the end result. In this example, proposals could be compared on a combination of variables. For example, on remuneration models (i.e., hourly rates or management fees), seeing what could be acquired within a certain budget, analysing which suppliers give the most for the investment, comparing the event attractiveness as presented by suppliers, reviewing past performance etc.

Buyers need to be proactive in supporting their internal clients when defining requirements. This is particularly true when budget holders have not developed the habit of collaborating with procurement. Since sourcing coverage is a challenge for many organizations, I have enclosed several recommendations to facilitate procurement acceptance by budget holders.

The implications of the needs identification phase for sales professionals follow this section. Sales processionals who are not used to dealing with procurement can review appendix 3 on page 97 which explains the proper attitude to adopt when procurement is suddenly part of the selling equation.

RECOMMENDATIONS FOR BUYERS

When an indirect procurement department is new, the relationships between buyers and budget holders have to be developed. Budget holders are likely to fear that procurement will delay their processes, will not take into consideration current suppliers' knowledge, and will only focus on costs. Additionally, budget holders may know more on procurement categories than new buyers and may wonder what procurement can bring to the equation.

As buyers, where should we start in such context?

Follow a Sourcing Process

New buyers with limited category expertise can simply follow the sequential sourcing process that is presented in this book.

When a "scope of work" (defining what is required) is completed with appropriate support from procurement, budget holders soon realize that questions from suppliers are less frequent, and the process is, in fact, faster. From my experience, if procurement does not get involved in defining needs (when acquiring indirect categories), it is likely to take longer before they manage to get involved in sourcing.

Following a rigorous process shows professionalism and is likely to inspire trust. As purchasers, you should be the one booking meetings and scheduling suppliers' visits along with budget holders (when relevant). Explaining the sourcing process at length is not recommended; emphasizing the added value and leading the process is the key.

Sell the Idea of Having Options

Stakeholders may believe that a sourcing process is not adequate, as the buyer may focus on price at the expense of quality. A good way to deal with this concern is to inform stakeholders that your objective as a buyer is to provide them with options. "Let's hear what suppliers have to recommend and in the end, we can choose what is best." I frequently use that argument to get people motivated.

Let the Budget Holder Make the Decision (Indirect)

Involving others in decision-making is the best way to avoid issues/complaints. In this way, suggestions and solutions become the focus, rather than the complaint. Allowing the budget holder to make decisions is sage advice. Procurement's role is to listen to budget holders and come up with recommendations to help influence decisions. With an open dialogue during the sourcing process, a consensus is generally reached.

Accept Not Covering All Purchases At First

Procurement has to build its expertise and deliver. To ensure meeting those objectives, it is best to first work with easier to source categories and more collaborative stakeholders.

Never Blame Budget Holders

As procurement professionals, we generally know when sourcing practices are adequate. It is best not to be hard on budget holders who do not act in the same way we do. A good strategy is to lead by example through success stories.

It is important not to burn bridges, but to show respect toward budget holders by leveraging their expertise. Without a budget holder's collaboration, no work can be done effectively. Sometimes, we can be wrong as well, so remaining professional can reduce the impact of mistakes.

Anyone with whom you collaborate has special talent and expertise. Recognizing those strengths is very useful and helps to establish relationships. For example, marketing people are generally very good at selling their projects internally, managing priorities, and being creative. The legal department's strengths include revising contracts and clarifying commercial agreements. Legal can flag when a commercial agreement is ambiguous or does not adequately protect the company. IT employees are generally very detail-oriented and can provide assistance when sourcing technical equipment, as well coming up with great saving opportunities. When relationships are good with all stakeholders, it helps to improve sourcing coverage and satisfaction toward procurement.

RECOMMENDATIONS FOR SALES PROFESSIONALS

The need identification phase represents the first strategic sourcing phase covered in this book. During this phase suppliers can sometime be involved for various reasons.

For example, purchasers may be looking for new sources of supply and for category insights. Buyers are generally interested in building knowledge on:

- The information that has to be provided to receive a quotation.

- What affects pricing

- How pricing should be broken down in an RFP

- What to be careful about when selecting a supplier

- The criteria that should be used to select a proposition

- Usual lead times to consider

- Who are the most promising suppliers etc.

On their side, budget holders are generally interested in understanding the services and how they are delivered; assessing compatibility between organizations, enquiring about costs, becoming motivated and reassured that new suppliers can deliver without needing too much direction from them.

Interacting with a purchaser can also be the result of a proactive supplier who manages to secure an introductory meeting to introduce its company.

In both cases, interacting with a potential client that is simply exploring the market or receptive to meet with a potential supplier offers a unique opportunity to eventually get invited to participate in an RFP and increase the odds of getting selected.

One of the main reason why these interactions are so important is because it is virtually impossible that any service related RFP be detailed enough to include everything that a customer will consider when it is time to select a proposition. One way to reduce this likely eventuality is to get to know the small details that are sometimes not communicated in a written RFP but are important in the selection decisions. Managing to engage with potential clients prior to formal tender processes can help gather such information. For example, a supplier offering event management services will certainly want to see pictures or videos of past events. This will allow understanding the customer standards.

Another reason why these interactions are important is because building trust with a new company that has never delivered before takes time and involves some risks. This is why, budget holders' preference is generally to remain with existing service providers. Resistance from budget holders can be worst when a potential client has been working with a same supplier for many years and when procurement has never sourced a specific service before. It offers a challenging context because budget holders may have become accustomed to having someone who knows them and what they want. This makes the process of explaining requirements difficult for them. When budget holders rotate positions frequently, it makes it even harder to describe requirements.

To cope with this reality, sale professionals will need to demonstrate that any transition would be smooth and supported by a professional. When approaching new clients, prospective suppliers are advised to explain the process they use to gather needs and ensure smooth delivery.

Meeting with potential clients can also provide the necessary motivation to issue a tender process. The usual context for this to happen is when buyers and budget holders believe that it would be beneficial to allow for more competition as a result of a greater awareness of potential superior suppliers

I have enclosed suggestions to maximize the outcomes of those introductory meetings.

Suggestions to Maximize the Outcome of Introductory Meetings:

When booking a meeting, it is recommended that you ask buyers or budget holders (when procurement is not involved) if other employees from the customer's side should be in attendance. For some categories, there might be several budget holders from different departments that may require a similar service. Good examples are printing services, translation and event management. Depending on the situation, a buyer may prefer to first meet with potential suppliers prior to engaging more resources. In such instances potential suppliers have an extra opportunity to learn about their client prior to meeting with decision makers (budget holders).

Suggesting an agenda and asking if there are special topics that the potential clients would like to cover during the meeting is often a good idea. Below are some suggested topics that could be presented:

- General information on the industry. Buyers and budget holders may appreciate attending a meeting to further their knowledge.

- Insights on vendors' selection. This may reveal weaknesses of current suppliers and trigger interests in running an RFP.

- Learning about cost drivers. Leveraging your expertise to help potential customers save money and/or control costs is likely to inspire trust.

- Information requirements to provide a quotation. The idea is to demonstrate that providing requirements to obtain a quotation is not complicated and is supported by an expert.

When a meeting is finally taking place, beginning by asking questions about the company and prospective customer roles (budget holder and buyer) is a great way to break the ice. In general, people like talking about themselves, so it makes everyone feel more comfortable. It should also spark reciprocal interest, so they ask more questions about you and your company.

During the meeting, sales professionals need to gather as much knowledge as possible from their potential clients.

Suggested Topics to Improve Knowledge of Potential Customers:

- Asking for an overview of the industry in which the potential client operates and information on the positioning of the company.

- Enquiring over usual requirements and frequencies. It is generally OK to ask for high-level figures to get an idea of the business potential.

- Enquiring as to how current services are executed.

- Asking if the potential customer usually deals with the same suppliers and if they tender most projects.

- Asking questions on current suppliers and satisfaction level.

- Asking for feedback on what is being presented. For example, if a supplier presents different products or services in different price ranges, getting input on what the customers relate to can be valuable.

Whenever possible and appropriate during introductory meetings, remind buyers and budget holders that you would love the opportunity to quote, even if no contract is secured. The last sentence "even if no contract is secured" is likely to help, as buyers will not feel locked in if a bidding process is not successful. Expressing a desire to quote indicates your interest in competing for business, which is aligned with one of the buyers' missions: reducing costs. Stating that providing a quotation can only serve the customer is a good lead-in. It is possible that a quotation is asked for to benchmark existing suppliers. Hopefully, this won't be the case, but rather, serves to secure an order. The key in helping facilitate this is to manage to demonstrate that any transition would be smooth and advantageous.

Sales professionals interested in getting more information on finding arguments to improve selling their services can review appendix 4 on page 98. A section on prospecting indirect customers is also available in appendix 5 on page 101.

2) MARKET ANALYSIS

For the purpose of this book, this chapter will be limited to the dynamic of searching for new suppliers and explaining how purchasers acquire knowledge of the supply market.

Researching for new suppliers is not an action that most buyers perform for every sourcing project. Looking for new suppliers is generally necessary when current suppliers do not have the required expertise or are deemed inadequate. It is much easier to work with existing service providers than introducing new ones. When looking for new suppliers is necessary, buyers will usually get insights from the following sources.

Common Ways to Find New Suppliers:

- Internal contacts (Procurement colleagues, budget holders, suppliers etc.)

Asking procurement colleagues to recommend new suppliers is effective, especially if they have already dealt with them. Another effective way to discover new suppliers is by asking budget holders. When their recommendations turn out to be good, it facilitates compliance. It also demonstrates that procurement is open to collaborating with whomever is best. Enquiring over the relationship between the budget holder and the suggested supplier is necessary to avoid conflicts of interest.

It is also possible to ask current reliable suppliers if they can recommend someone else to perform a new service that is outside of their scope. Sometimes current suppliers might offer to extend their services. Hiring existing suppliers can turn out to be an effective strategy, as they already know the customer, and it is often surprising how competitive they can be.

Websites

The web offers an easy way to discover new suppliers. Most of the time, web searches require phone calls to obtain more information and assess suppliers' compatibility.

Issuing an RFI

The formal way to discover suppliers and obtain more details on a service is through an RFI. It requires identifying potential suppliers through various means and sending an official document with questions. RFI are important as they serve to acquire knowledge and identify potential suppliers. Entrepreneurs and sales representatives should definitely take this seriously because it usually allows for more interaction with buyers, and sometimes budget holders, than when answering a request for tender.

When buyers receive a lot of support from a potential supplier during an RFI, it is likely to help build trust.

Enquiring from purchasing associations

Procurement associations can provide insight on a broad range of sourcing topics and networking opportunities to facilitate purchasers' roles.

These organizations normally charge annual fees and provide procurement related information, which can be accessed and shared with members.

The Chartered Institute of Procurement & Supply (CIPS) from the UK is the world's largest procurement and supply professional organisation. CIPS has a global community of over 110,000 members in 150 different countries.

IFPSM is a global standard setter for the profession of purchasing and supply management, providing leadership to the profession and setting a benchmark for professional excellence. This organization reaches 250,000 procurement professionals internationally.

The Institute for Supply Management® (ISM®) is committed to advancing the practice of supply management to drive value and competitive advantage for its members. ISM is an innovator and leader in the profession through the renowned ISM Report On Business®, highly regarded certification programs, and industry-standard training and educational resources. ISM maintains a strong global influence, serving professionals in the supply chain across more than 90 countries.

In Canada, the Supply Chain Management Association (SCMA) is the Canadian representative of (IFPSM), and they offer a globally recognized certification, called SCMP (Supply Chain Management Professional designation).

There are also private associations that focus on large international companies. For example, Procurement Leaders is a membership organization that provides its network with category and strategy intelligence. It has offices in the US, UK, Australia, and India.

COMPARING SUPPLIERS

In the market analysis phase, buyers are searching for the most promising suppliers to participate in a tender process and gain market and category knowledge. For efficiency purpose, buyers will generally develop pre selection criteria to shortlist suppliers who will then be invited to participate in a tender process.

Budget holders generally don't spend much coming up with selection criteria. It is the buyer's job to ensure that its customers (budget holders) have all the necessary information to make the best rational decision and lead this phase. From a buyer's standpoint, the easiest way to contribute to developing these criteria is to put yourself in the position of a budget holder, and selecting a supplier based on your needs. This simple exercise is enough to figure out most pre-selection and selection criteria. Once the criteria are developed, buyers have to validate them and agree on a prorating with the support of a budget holder (Indirect Procurement).

Selection criteria are likely to change throughout this phase as buyers and budget holders learn new information. For example, a budget holder may express a preference for a software provider that has a local office to limit travel costs. If the market analysis reveals that local suppliers are not adequate, this criterion becomes less relevant.

Suppliers need to understand that buyers and budget holders are not necessarily experts at sourcing the product or services that suppliers specialize in.

This is why it is important to put yourself in your customers' shoes. For example, if a long-term supplier who has become accustomed to getting business without having to respond to RFPs or RFQs is suddenly being asked to quote against competitors, then simply expecting that the customer's logical choice will be you is not the right approach.

The recommended approach is to be as helpful as possible, so the buyers are able to compare suppliers based on relevant information pertaining to the category. Doing this extra work helps to build trust. This help will not necessarily be asked for directly, but when a supplier manages to educate potential customers, it increases the odds of making a good impression and getting selected.

For example, in a complex IT project, I decided to allow all suppliers participating in the tender process to comment on a complex price response template. Some suppliers made no recommendation, other little recommendations, and one made a lot of recommendations. It is evident which supplier seemed more eager to help the customer. Amongst others, suggestions to avoid surprises (possible extras) were appreciated.

Using a pricing template to answer an RFP is strongly suggested, as understanding and comparing complex quotations can turn out to be very challenging.

Now let's review the third stage, purchasing strategies.

3) Purchasing Strategies

At this stage, buyers know what they have to source, which suppliers to invite to a tender process, and have a good understanding of how to select the offer that best fits the requirements.

Developing purchasing strategies means thinking of ways to obtain maximum benefits for the organization. For instance, if the main objective were to reduce costs, then inviting multiple suppliers to quote would make sense. It is best to develop purchasing strategies prior to issuing tender documents, so it is taken into consideration in the RFQs/RFPs structure. For example, if one of the objectives is to reduce the risks associated with defective products, then it would make sense to plan a question on warranties and prorate the selection criteria accordingly. It is difficult to foresee all opportunities that could come up during a tender process, but planning helps.

I have listed some examples of purchasing strategies to better illustrate what it means.

Purchasing Strategies Examples:

Breaking down costs

This strategy focuses on comparing proposals on many aspects to increase negotiation leverage through enhanced transparency.

Inviting new suppliers to quote

This strategy focuses on expanding tender opportunities to new suppliers to increase competition.

Challenging the effectiveness of products or services

Sometimes, it can be very difficult to negotiate when budget holders are eager to secure products or services, and suppliers add pressure by stating limited availability. In such situations, buyers may need to further their analysis if they wish to gain some negotiating leverage.

For example, in some media deals I negotiated, I challenged the cost of different media products (i.e., a banner versus a digital screen) by enquiring on the cost per impression (price paid for each potential clients that see an add). The analysis revealed that different suppliers had different ways of calculating their cost per impression. It also turned out that the cost of each media product was not entirely linked to their effectiveness. This kind of analysis was useful during negotiations.

Bluffing

It is possible that only one supplier can deliver a product or a service. In this case, advising suppliers that there are other viable options may be a good strategy. Some sort of bluffing can also be used during benchmarking exercises. Getting an overall idea of the cost for a service provides some guidance, but sometimes there are just too many details that would need to be analyzed to come up with exact numbers. When a sourcing team is unable to know all the details it can happen that high-level figures are used to obtain price concessions.

Subcontracting specific components

When buyers receive a cost breakdown, they can evaluate if some sub-components could be sourced elsewhere to reduce total costs (the tender document should outline this possibility). This strategy can also add risks.

For example, in a project to acquire price signs, a supplier stated that one component was no longer available from the former supplier. Sourcing this component from another source would mean heavy price increase. What I did in this project was to enquire on the cost of that component from the last order. I then asked another supplier that I knew could get almost anything to look for a supplier that could produce this component. It turned that we were able to get that component and reduce the total order cost by 30 %, which was significant. The downside was that it took a bit longer than expected and the price sign provider was critical of the quality of the component. On our side we were satisfied with the quality.

Extending commitment in exchange for extended terms

This strategy consists of investigating if suppliers would be willing to offer discounts in exchange for extended terms.

Buying product substitutes

This strategy consists of investigating if different products could be used. For example, metal parts can be made from raw material or by using metal powder (high volume).

Sourcing from lower-cost countries

This can be achieved by evaluating if leveraging lower salaries in alternative countries could save money. Lead-time, quality, and reputation must be maintained.

Aggregating Volume

There is a tendency for organizations to concentrate volume with a limited number of suppliers to obtain better conditions.

To conclude with this section, purchasing strategies are not set; buyers have to tailor their strategies to each situation. When both budget holders and procurement become more familiar with certain services and suppliers, it is possible to improve strategies over time. When developing purchasing strategies, it is important to gather the facts and trust your business instincts. It is also highly recommended that you seek opinions from budget holders and other partners (i.e. a marketing agency) to ensure alignment.

4) Market Approaches, Request for Proposals (RFPs), Request for Quotations (RFQs)

Formal RFPs and/or RFQs are usually issued when companies want to obtain bids in formal ways. Another way to obtain bids is by simply asking suppliers to quote without necessarily sending official documents. Requesting non-formal quotations can be done by e-mail or by phone. One of the disadvantages of quick informal quotation requests is that the rules of engagement are not communicated right from the outset. This can cause issues later on.

As an example, I had once requested several quotes over the phone to source a fax to e-mail service for an urgent pilot. I did not use a formal tender document stipulating rules on price validity period. A supplier was selected based on flexibility and cheaper service. Quickly after beginning the commercial relationship, we learned that the previously mentioned price was no longer valid. I had been less cautious during this process because initially, we were piloting a solution, which I believed could be modified if necessary. When I learned from the budget holder that it was no longer possible to switch due to internal constraints, I was stuck and I had to explain to the budget holder why I was unable to fix the situation.

This situation could have been avoided by including a price validity protection clause along with my initial request. Obviously, not honouring price is not a great way to start a business relationship with a new customer. It is pretty rare that companies cannot change their minds during a so-called "pilot." Regarding this specific situation, I was able to negotiate a good rate later on, when we reached a level where budget holders were willing to finally switch to another supplier. Since staying with the current supplier remained the easiest option (no transition costs and hassle), it was decided to pursue the relationship at a reasonable cost.

Below are presented standards elements that can be found in tender documents (RFPs and RFQs).

Standard Information Contained in RFPs and RFQs:

Description of the Company Issuing the Sourcing Document

The objective is to provide high-level information on the company issuing a tender.

Products or Services Requirements

For production goods, the requirements may be item numbers or technical drawings. For a service, requirements are often a description of what is required.

Roles and Responsibilities

Clarifying roles and responsibilities is more relevant for RFPs than RFQs and is used to help stakeholders better understand their respective roles.

Taking proper time to define roles and responsibilities is a topic that could well be brought up by suppliers, instead of relying on proactive buyers. For example, a supplier that had won an RFP could certainly benefit from clarifying who does what via a role and responsibilities chart. Focusing on operational details improves the chances that expectations are met and opens the door to improving efficiency. For instance, if both the supplier and the budget holder are doing a similar monthly report, then one of the two could stop doing so.

No Obligations to Buy

It is recommended that you add clauses stating that participating in an RFP or an RFQ does not imply any obligations to award a contract or compensate the company for the efforts and possible amendments.

While this may not seem necessary to many, I have experienced a couple of situations where suppliers made requests to be compensated or complained when they learned that a sourcing process was cancelled. I have also come across suppliers who became used to getting repetitive business, and complained when price requests did not result in business for them.

Over time, sole-sourced suppliers may come to believe that asking for a price means placing an order. To avoid unpleasant requests from suppliers, no obligation to buy and no compensation for modifications or cancellations clauses can be added, even during non-formal purchasing requests. Complaints related to the previous example usually leave a bad impression. Thus, complaining when a request is cancelled or awarded to another supplier is not recommended. Obviously, if the process does not appear to be fair, it can be discussed in a constructive manner.

Timeline

This section describes when sourcing stages are expected to occur. Buyers and budget holders do not necessarily know what reasonable timelines are. When there is a concern over the timeline, it should be discussed openly with buyers. Most of the time, all suppliers quoting will express timeline concerns when it is not reasonable.

Delays in submitting a quotation can occur due to a current suppliers' workload. This should be discussed, and usually companies will accommodate if they can. Since large companies often deal with a limited number of suppliers, they tend to be accommodating. When buyers cannot extend a tender deadline, they will still appreciate being informed if it may cause issues. Buyers need to be certain that the supplier they select can deliver. This should not limit future bidding opportunities when explanations are provided.

Buyer's Coordinates

Contact information is communicated to bidders in the event that it becomes necessary to ask questions or to simply reply to tenders. Not contacting anyone else is important, unless permission is granted from the purchaser.

There are several reasons communications are centralized, such as:

- To treat all suppliers equally by communicating similar information to all suppliers

- To avoid leaking of confidential information

Q&A Process

Adding a period for suppliers to ask questions offers the opportunity to clarify expectations equally with all suppliers. Ideally, suppliers should submit all questions in writing, as they are usually shared with other suppliers participating in a tender process. This ensures that all suppliers bid on the same requirements. From a buyer's standpoint, sharing questions also signals there is competition.

Buyers should use their judgment in deciding which questions should or shouldn't be shared. For example, good ideas that would give a competitive advantage to a supplier quoting should not necessarily be shared with other suppliers. Information explaining the requirements should.

Making Recommendations During the Q&A Process

When a supplier receives an RFP or an RFQ request and believes that relevant questions are missing for the customer to make the right decision, they could leverage the Q&A process to make suggestions. Although tender documents may not end up amended, it will demonstrate that the supplier is proactive and collaborative.

If there is no formal Q&A process described in the sourcing documents (RFP or RFQ), buyers could still appreciate getting insight if important questions are not being asked. If recommendations are made, they should be done quickly after receiving the tender documents. For example, this type of question is likely to be appreciated:

"Do you think that asking for this information would help make a better comparison? We believe that it would be important for you to evaluate this important aspect."

When a tender process is over, it is too late to make recommendations. It is important to remember that buyers cannot be experts at everything they source, so appropriate support is likely to inspire trust.

I once ran an RFP that had to be issued twice, because the first one did not properly address our needs. Before the second RFP was sent, a supplier suggested that we ask when the last printer models were developed to ensure buying up-to-date technology. I found this information relevant and thought it would have been useful to know during the first RFP.

Proposals' Price Validity Period

As per a previous example, this clause informs bidders that prices should remain valid for a certain period. Since the sourcing process for important acquisitions can take several months, it is important not to face unexpected price increases once an order is finally placed.

Payment Term

This is to inform suppliers how long it will take before they get paid. Suppliers rarely comment on payment terms, but it is important to add a note explaining that this element will need further discussion should it cause an issue.

It is problematic when a supplier gets selected and then comes back with different payment terms. In fact, this should not ever happen when it is clarified in the tender documents.

Insurance Coverage

Proof of insurance coverage and/or specific coverage requirements may be requested.

Warranties

It is recommended for procurement to share expectations in terms of product durability, spare parts availability, and expected warranties. Stating how long a product is expected to last can definitely impact quality recommendations and costs.

Proactive suppliers could benefit from clarifying expectations when there are no guidelines. This is rarely done, but can offer an edge in terms of getting back with the right offer.

Termination Clauses

Sometimes, companies have to cancel orders after a contract has been awarded. As a general rule, orders can be cancelled, but the supplier must be paid for the completed work or delivered products. This is called a termination for convenience. Suppliers are strongly advised to clarify shall they intend to charge penalties in case a contract got cancelled prior to its term. This will facilitate resolution and reduce conflicts.

Having to pay a penalty when an order is cancelled or reduced is sometimes normal. For example, a company that has leased a car for four years will have to pay a penalty if the car is returned after one year only. Another example could be a supplier who had to invest in production equipment for a specific customer.

Customers may decide to terminate a contract due to a breach of contract. This is called termination for cause. To facilitate terminating a contract for cause, a signed contract should contain reasons for terminations for cause and usually allow a time frame to correct issues.

Right to Audit

This clause would allow companies to perform audits at the supplier's location. Clearly, good reasons would be needed to perform an audit. This clause should not be refused as it leaves a bad impression.

Best Price Clause

This clause stipulates that suppliers should offer the same competitive price as they charge other similar customers. In reality, this clause is difficult to enforce, but it rings an alarm bell when a supplier is opposed to it.

Selection Criteria

In the market analysis phase, we have seen how preselection and selection criteria are identified. In tender documents, it is good practice for purchasers to share the final selection criteria. These criteria can be clearly listed or reflected in the questions that suppliers have to respond to.

In the event that selection criteria are not clearly expressed in tender documents, suppliers should ask buyers what they are.

Buyers may not share selection criteria with weighting. Personally, I prefer not to give the weighting, as important information may only be discovered during a tender process. Additionally, the weighting can prove to be inadequate when analysing proposals. In my opinion, the weighting should be followed closely and serve as a guideline to allow debating and decision-making.

I have enclosed an example below.

In this example, there are six selection criteria, two of which cannot be weighted, as they are mandatory. This example was simplified for explanation purposes.

The internal customer has a budget limit of $110,000 that is not disclosed to suppliers.

Evaluation results:

Suppliers have been evaluated on four criteria using a scale of 1 to 5, 5 being the highest score. The price ratings come from a formula. In this example, supplier 3 has the highest prorated score with 3,90.

Criteria	Prorating	Supplier 1	Supplier 2	Supplier 3
(Scale from 1 to 5, 5 equal highest score)				
Company's experience dealing with similar clients	0.1	4	5	3
Price	0.6	4	1	5
Recommended solutions	0.3	3	5	2
Ability to meet deadline – Mandatory		Yes	Yes	Yes
Proper insurance coverage – Mandatory		Yes	Yes	Yes
Prorated score:		3.55	2.38	3.90

Prices	100 000 $	150 000 $	80 000 $
Price rating* (see cost formula below)	4	1	5

Figure 14

The cost formula that was used to calculate the price rating can be found below. [13]

Cost Formula for Price Rating

$$1 - \left(\frac{B - A}{A}\right) X\ C = D$$

Figure 15

"The cost criterion is rated by awarding the proposal with the lowest total cost the maximum number of Cost points available. The remaining proposals are rated by applying the following formula:

A—the lowest Offer's supplier' cost.

B—the Offeror's cost being scored.

C—the maximum number of cost points available.

D—Offeror's cost scores (points).

Note: If the formula results in a negative number (which will occur when the Offeror's cost is more than twice the lowest cost), zero points shall be assigned."

In this example, if the buyer sticks with the prorated evaluation criteria results, the business would be awarded to supplier 3, who has the highest score. However, the budget holder has a preference for the second supplier's proposal that is off budget by $40,000.

Supplier 2 may simply be overpriced or may not have properly understood the requirements. When there are huge price discrepancies between proposals, it is best for buyers to carry out checks. However, let's not assume that all buyers will push further their investigations. For this reason, it is important not to leave any room for ambiguity.

For example, it is recommended that suppliers always sum up numbers, clarify what is an option and what is not. If not already required, detailing all cost is also recommended as it inspires trust and can avoid misinterpretations.

One way to check whether a proposal is easy to understand is to ask someone with no knowledge of the products or services for feedback.

Response Templates

Responding to RFPs is quite similar to responding to RFQs, but there is likely to be a higher proportion of non-financial criteria/questions. To facilitate comparing proposals, buyers are advised to ask suppliers to complete pre-defined pricing response templates and non-financial response templates. Without predefined response templates, the risk of mistakes is high. Buyers spend more time analysing proposals than other stakeholders, and sometimes they only provide RFP response summaries. For this reason, if ever there is a misunderstanding in a proposition, it is likely to remain unnoticed. When no response templates are provided, as a minimum, there should be a required response sequence to follow.

For buyers, well-detailed response templates provide bargaining power and a better understanding of what is being acquired. In my opinion, knowledge is crucial when it comes to negotiation. When there is competition, buyers are in a privileged position to negotiate because they have reviewed multiple proposals which the sales side could not do. With this significant advantage, negotiating from a buyer's standpoint does not solely depend on the negotiation strategies gleaned from many sales books, but mainly on facts.

You will find below an example demonstrating the importance of developing well-detailed response templates to capture and compare proposals.

Comparing Prices Without Pre-Defined Pricing Templates:

In this example, two suppliers are quoting for a trade show booth. Costs are not linked to the previous example.

Last year's cost

$105,000

Current year quotations:

Supplier 1 response:

Activities	Costs
Trade booth	$70,000
Animation	$3,000
Rental	$40,000

Total: $113,000

Figure 16

69

Supplier 2 response:

Activities	Costs
Trade booth set-up and dismantle	$15,000
Animation	$5,000
Rental	$40,000
Lighting and sound	$12,000
Transportation fees	$18,000
Warehousing	$8,000

Total: $98,000

Figure 17

Non-Financial Observations

Budget holders prefer supplier 1's trade booth design, but due to price differentiation and budget constraints, supplier 2 seems more appropriate.

Recognizing that it is difficult to compare proposals, the proactive buyer asks the first supplier to split costs according to the second supplier's breakdown and asks for additional explanations.

Comparison According to a Similar Pricing Template

Activities	Supplier 1	Supplier 2	% Difference
Trade booth set-up and dismantle	$12,000	$15,000	20.00%
Animation	$10,000 (6 promo staff)	$5,000 (3 promo staff)	-100.00%
Rental	$31,000	$40,000	22.50%
Lighting and sound	$20,000	$12,000	-66.67%
Transportation fees	$25,000	$18,000	-38.89%
Warehousing	$15,000	$8,000	-87.50%
Total:	**$113,000**	**$98,000**	

Figure 18

Comparisons Between Proposals:

- Supplier 1 has a nicer booth (more appealing)
- Supplier 1 quoted for 6 promo staff when only 3 are needed
- Supplier 1 has cheaper rental costs
- Supplier 1 lighting budget could be reduced without reducing the impact
- Supplier 1 has higher transportation fees
- Supplier 1 quoted much higher warehousing fees

In the RFP response, supplier 1 mentioned they don't have access to competitive logistics rates, but suggested that the customer's logistics provider handle this part.

After consulting the internal logistics department, it was found that this service could be handled internally for $6,500.

Revised Costs

Following a more detailed analysis, supplier one is being asked to modify its bid to align with initial requirements

Quotation update

- Revisions in staff capacity for supplier 1 from 10k to 5K

- Reduced lighting budget for supplier 1 from 20k to 15K

- Reduced transportation fees for suppliers 1 and 2 at the internal cost of 6.5K

Activities	Supplier 1	Supplier 2	% Difference
Trade booth set-up and dismantle	$12,000	$15,000	20.00%
Animation (3 promo staff)	$5,000	$5,000	-100.00%
Rental	$31,000	$40,000	22.50%
Lighting and sound	$15,000	$12,000	-66.67%
Transportation fees	$6,500	$6,500	-38.89%
Warehousing	$15,000	$8,000	-87.50%

Total: $84,500 $86,500

Figure 19

By simply breaking down costs, asking for clarifications, and using supplier 1's logistic recommendation, costs were reduced by 20% (supplier 1) compared with last year's baseline. Although this percentage seems high, it is definitely achievable.

When breaking down costs between suppliers, buyers are in a good bargaining position. In this example, it would be easy to challenge supplier 1 on warehousing fees ($15,000 compared with $8,000). Assuming that it was done, the final price for supplier 1 could probably be reduced to around $78,000.

Through improved transparency and knowledge sharing, supplier 1 managed to secure the contract, despite being more expensive at first.

If the buyer had simply asked supplier 1 to be more competitive without any further understanding of the proposal, it would not have produced the same result. For example, a buyer could have simply negotiated with supplier 1, because it had a nicer booth and accepted a deal closer to the second supplier's pricing.

To avoid lengthy back and forth and potential mistakes, the ideal would have been to include a well-detailed pricing template (like the second supplier pricing breakdown) when the buyer drafted the RFP. With this example, one can conclude that the buyer did not do a good job with the initial pricing template nor with describing staff and lighting requirements.

Additional Information That Can Help Getting Selected

Response templates may not include all relevant questions that buyers and budget holders would like to know. By adding optional information, entrepreneurs and sales representatives can display their proposition strengths and potentially impact sourcing decisions.

Recommendations

As mentioned earlier, suppliers have a tendency to respond to exactly what is being asked for. When a supplier knows different ways to achieve objectives, it can certainly be communicated when responding to a tender request. The way to do that is to first answer what is being requested and add a section with recommendations.

For some suppliers, recommendations could be as simple as suggesting using different materials or showing the impact of allowing more time to execute a project. Budget holders sometimes ask for earlier than necessary delivery deadlines to cover for possible delays.

Making recommendations can make a difference. Whenever a potential customer wonders, "Why have I never been told this by my usual supplier?" it helps to secure business. It also makes your offer appear superior when the recommendations are good.

Commercial Incentives

As previously discussed, potential suppliers should quote according to what is being asked, but nothing forbids them from offering incentives to potentially increase sales. For example, it can be beneficial to offer discounts in exchange for longer-term commitments, volume discounts, or additional services free of charge.

It can also be a good strategy to keep some of these incentives for post tender negotiations. Post tender negotiations happen when a supplier is close to being selected, but final details need to be negotiated prior to awarding a deal.

Internal Processes

Buyers and budget holders appreciate knowing that a supplier is well organized. This is why it could be useful to elaborate on major internal processes. This can be done during introductory meetings, suppliers' presentations and/or in written responses to RFQs and RFPs.

For example, a company that has to deliver error-free products would benefit from displaying robust quality control processes to reassure potential customers.

Supplier Performance

It is appreciated when a supplier adds a section on supplier performance. In this section, the supplier can suggest KPIs with targets and a time frame for performance reviews. It is suggested that they add a note stating that KPIs are recommendations and can be modified to meet customers' needs.

KPIs for direct goods usually contain standard measurements, such as on-time delivery, quality, quantity and price. These KPIs can sometime be automatically calculated by customers' ERP systems.

Measuring performance for services (Indirect procurement) usually involves a manual process, is more subjective and can be delicate. A good example of subjectivity is when a new employee, who has never dealt with a previous supplier, is being asked to rate performance. In this case, it could be that all employees that have had experience dealing with the old supplier find the new one just perfect. On the other hand, a new employee would not be in a position to appreciate improvements or not yet able to understand the challenges.

An example of a delicate evaluation would be a marketing agency being evaluated on its ability to deliver. If the customer has caused delays, it could be delicate to let them know who is responsible for these issues.

References

It is recommended that you include contact details of satisfied customers along with reference letters. References are not always validated by phone, and it is unlikely that all stakeholders will participate when calling for feedback. By sharing recommendation letters, it is easier for all members of the selection committee to have access to the same information. Sharing references from clients on the purchasing side is recommended when presenting to procurement as these references will be more relevant to this department.

BCP (Business Continuity Plan)

Suppliers that are qualified as "less strategic" are probably not required to demonstrate they have contingency plans in place to cope with elements that could disrupt service delivery.

Although it is most often not a requirement, it looks good to demonstrate the measures put in place to avoid service interruptions.

Variables Impacting Costs

Listing variables that may impact cost is a good way to reduce possible surprises. Adding this information can also help customers ensure they have accounted for all possibilities when describing requirements.

For example, a supplier once told me he acquired new business from an internal budget holder referral. The supplier quoted on a project and got selected. After his bid was selected, he had been asked for modifications and was told that no additional budget was available when the topic of additional fees came up. He asked me what I thought.

My recommendation was to accept the deal if he was still making money. Once budgets are approved, it is not always ideal/feasible to request additional funds. To avoid this from happening again, I suggested that next time he shares variables impacting costs.

Now, let's review the next phase that usually occurs when sourcing services or complex products: the proposal presentation.

5) Proposal Presentation

Depending on the nature of what is being sourced, buyers and budget holders (when appropriate) may require suppliers to present and explain their proposal.

Presenting a proposal usually represents an opportunity for new suppliers, as existing suppliers usually invest less effort. Most of the time, they assume the customer already knows their capabilities. Although this is true, it does negatively affect their evaluation. In addition, budget holders report to other people, and they like presenting nice material from suppliers to explain their projects and choices.

Why request a presentation?

- To fully understand a proposition

- To learn new information that was not covered in the written documents

- To address last minute questions

- To assesses compatibility between employees

- To evaluate the probability that the selected supplier delivers smoothly

- To evaluate the supplier's integrity and get assurances that there won't be surprises once a supplier has been selected

Unspoken Needs

For new suppliers, presenting a proposal offers a good opportunity to demonstrate a thorough understanding of the customer's expectations.

This means not only responding to the RFP or RFQ questions, but also covering what is important to the customer. The idea is to demonstrate that the supplier truly understands what has to be done and how it will be done to reassure customers. This will be necessary to reduce internal resistance in dealing with a new supplier.

Pleasing Everyone

During the presentation, it is important to please everyone, especially the employees who will benefit from the service or product on a daily basis. It is important to show respect, even when questions appear obvious or redundant. Remember, your customers are not necessarily experts in your field of expertise. Being arrogant can screw up the entire deal.

Similar to introductory meetings, but even more relevant when responding to a tender process, bringing key people to present can facilitate a connection with the selection committee members (when there is one). Matching expertise expectations is a good strategy. For example, if the budget holder is a technical person, then a technical person from your organisation should attend. If the customer is from marketing, then an employee familiar with marketing could be helpful. These details can make a difference. Be sure to inform the buyer of how many people will be in attendance, so an appropriate room can be booked.

Companies that are shortlisted usually stand a relatively good chance of being selected, so every small detail counts. Decisions between two proposals are sometimes difficult to make. For instance, if the committee is not unanimously convinced, a vote by a show of hands may close discussions. In that case, each member has equal say.

As already discussed, getting a new indirect supplier on board can prove to be difficult due to internal resistance. When an indecisive selection committee is faced with two proposals, it may be advantageous for buyers to seize the opportunity to get a new supplier on board when the opportunity arises. This decision can increase leverage to negotiate later on. The reason I am bringing this up is to remind you of how important it is for existing service providers to maintain good relationships with all stakeholders, including procurement!

Sometimes a supplier is not selected right away due to internal resistance, but good suppliers usually manage to secure business over time.

Tender Document Sequence

When answering an RFP or an RFQ, it is important to follow the sourcing document sequence. Buyers and budget holders appreciate it when the sequence is being followed, as it facilitates easier comparison of proposals. Surprisingly, it is quite common for suppliers not to respect the sequence but use their own.

In the event that an RFP or RFQ does not require a sequence, this should offer a good opportunity to engage with buyers and ask if they have special requirements.

Rehearsal

Rehearsing for a presentation can significantly improve the chances of being selected. What presenters are trying to communicate and how it is perceived can be very different.

Practicing with people who are less familiar with the topic, is a good way to see if your message is being delivered effectively. This is extremely relevant because the people who will rate suppliers are not necessarily experts at buying what is presented. Other buyers from suppliers' organisations could also provide great insight since they have a different perspective. Initial impressions are hard to change, so it is best to get it right the first time.

Leaving Hard Copies

At the end of the presentation, providing hard copies of your presentation is recommended, as it allows the buyers to revisit the proposal easily. When the documentation is nicely presented, it also leaves a good impression.

6) Supplier Selection & Post Tender Negotiations

Supplier's Selection

Once all proposals have been received, analysed, and clarified, the selection committee selects a supplier.

Although a choice is almost final, it is possible that further negotiations on terms and conditions, price, payment terms etc., are conducted prior to closing a deal. Most of the time, these negotiations occur with the supplier who has the most chances of getting selected. Less frequently, it could happen that some aspects are discussed with more than one supplier when the final choice depends on final negotiations.

More often than not, the supplier's choice is evident, and an evaluation grid can be seen as a formality, but it is definitely good practice to use one. The evaluation grid is a useful tool to help make rational decisions, provide feedback to selected and non-selected suppliers, and document decisions.

Suppliers who have submitted their bid are usually actively looking for feedback. My recommendation is not to add unnecessary pressure, unless an urgent commitment is required to deliver as per the customer timeline. As a buyer, I would love to pick up the phone the minute I know which supplier is selected, but it would be unwise to do so. Buyers and budget holders have to make sure that all possible questions and validations are completed before announcing a winner. Not doing so may jeopardise buyers' leverage in case of last-minute modifications and negotiations.

When there is a strong confidence in the selected supplier and the assurance that no surprises will crop up should they receive indication that they will be awarded with a contract, it becomes possible to be more transparent toward the end of the process. For instance, if resources have to be booked in advance, giving a heads up may be necessary.

For example, on a sourcing project with an IT service provider from Poland, the selection committee felt secure that the supplier would not take advantage of any situations. Building trust had been achieved through all the constructive interactions, starting from an RFI process, followed by proactive feedback during discovery sessions, an RFP process and by validating references of existing customers. Cost overruns with IT software projects are quite frequent due to the challenges of expressing needs.

As opposed to other bidders and due to their extensive expertise, the selected IT supplier stated that they would absorb any unforeseen surprises, because they were confident that they understood what had to be done. No other suppliers competing for business mentioned willingness to absorb any additional costs.

Post Tender Negotiations

Most of the time, private companies will conduct post tender negotiations. As mentioned, negotiation is usually conducted with the most promising supplier, following a tender process. Buyers are often in a good position to negotiate because of all the steps (sourcing process) that they have been through. Comparing multiple proposals with detailed response templates helps during negotiation.

The propensity to negotiate can be influenced by several factors such as: buyers/budget holders' personalities, saving objectives, opportunities, corporate culture, levels of competition, competitiveness of the offer etc.

Buyers' Personalities

Some buyers may negotiate for the sake of negotiating, while others pay attention to small details and find justified reasons to negotiate. Some buyers or budget holders are naturally aggressive when it comes to negotiation, while others are more cooperative and reasonable.

Buyers' Saving Targets

Savings targets typically fluctuate between three and six percent annually on addressable spending. When involved, budget holders (indirect) may appreciate paying good rates as per the RFP and simply hope that buyers attempt to improve commercial conditions. In other words, further gains are not always a necessary prerequisite before awarding a contract, but it can help smooth relationships with purchasers that have saving targets to meet.

The reality is that buyers' saving targets do not take into consideration the fact that prices obtained during tenders may already be fair and competitive. This is why negotiation is likely to occur.

In my opinion, negotiations are more likely to occur for new products and services. The reason being that the baseline is taken from the RFP or RFQ rates. It is generally easier to find better deals for products or services that have already been sourced.

Level of Competition

When competition is high and many suppliers are able to offer similar products or services, it is easier to negotiate. To distinguish service offering, it is recommended that suppliers not only focus on what they sell, but ascertain how to make their customers' lives easier.

Should Suppliers Make Concessions During Post Negotiation?

Unfortunately, there is no straightforward answer to this question, as it depends on the situation. The situation could be that lowering rates is necessary; requests have been made to several bidders, and the one that accepts will secure the contract. Alternatively, only one supplier has been asked for improvements, and negotiating is not mandatory, as price is already competitive; a budget holder may not care about getting better rates.

One way to assess how serious a buyer is would be to listen to the arguments. When the only argument is "sharpen your pencil" without further explanations, making concessions is less justified. When good reasons are provided, then analyzing the request further is recommended. Making reasonable concessions shows flexibility, which is appreciated and can lead to benefits.

Should sales professionals decide to collaborate before making unnecessary concessions, my advice would be to ask the purchaser what concessions are most important to obtain during negotiations. It could be getting free products or services, getting price volume discounts, negotiating a global deal, obtaining better pricing, longer payment terms, improving warranties, or investing in an efficiency initiative. It is recommended that you tell them that you will investigate what can be done, but you cannot commit at this point.

Some buyers are just not reasonable when it comes to negotiating.

For example, a procurement colleague related a story about an aggressive purchaser, who requested that a long time supplier forget some past invoices in order to retain business. My colleague was in shock, because she felt that it was unfair, but was also surprised to hear that the deal was accepted. When the request is not reasonable, it does not have to be accepted. Large companies (customers) also have a reputation to protect.

When the requested concessions are exaggerated, I would recommend booking a meeting with the purchaser to discuss. If the buyer is eager to accept lower concessions early on, it could mean that the negotiations were not necessarily mandatory for you to be awarded the deal. The benefit of this approach is that the buyer will remember your professional approach and recognize that if they hope to save next time, they will need to invest time and meet with you instead of closing a deal in a matter of minutes with a simple phone call.

Whenever negotiations are conducted, they should be executed respectfully, so the buyer is never motivated to find alternative solutions. Thinking of creative and innovative ways to trade savings for added value is the recommended approach of this book, because it produces far better results than solely asking for better prices.

When there is a saving, buyers will have to calculate and report how much was saved, as this KPI is definitely important. To calculate, buyers will need to show two quotations or agreements and demonstrate the cost variance between the initial and revised document. Savings can also be reported with a small sentence from a supplier such as: "as agreed with Mister X, a discount of X% representing $X was applied to the quotation." Help from suppliers is appreciated.

Possible Advantages To Accept Negotiating

- It can improve the relationship with the buyer.

- Buyers have a referral role; they will be more inclined to recommend a supplier that shows a bit of flexibility and helps them achieve their own objectives.

- The name of the supplier and the savings will be displayed on a savings report, thus increasing the possibility of becoming or remaining at the top of people's minds for other buyers and management.

- It can speed-up the approval process.

- Greater commitment from procurement when there are issues, such as late payments, satisfaction issues, internal stakeholders not collaborating, compliance with the deal etc.

Given the advantages of accepting the offer to negotiate, I think in most cases, showing flexibility is recommended. When a supplier truly believes their costs should not be lowered, I would still recommend looking for efficiency savings or, at least, explaining the position carefully.

In the event that a budget holder (indirect procurement) is strongly supporting negotiations, there is extra reason to show flexibility. From my experience, when budget holders are aligned with buyers on seeking better prices, there is a greater chance for non-collaborative and unreasonable suppliers to eventually get replaced.

I do not expect all readers to agree with my position with respect to negotiations, but as this book states, this is the buyer's perspective with the intent of remaining neutral.

I have experienced suppliers, who had no reason to negotiate and did not due to their privileged positions (monopolistic positions). Having done so, these "privileged" suppliers have lost more in the long-run and failed to remain on top indefinitely. For example, the suppliers with unique strengths on core products or services do not necessarily have that position on non-core products or services. As a result, buyers and budget holders will do whatever they can to source these secondary items or services from other suppliers or reassess needs on a continuous basis to avoid unnecessary spending.

One way to reduce the likelihood of buyers asking for concessions is to be proactive. As we saw earlier, suppliers that contribute and track their savings are seen as already contributing. Why not come up with recommendations, be seen as proactive, and be at the top of people's mind, so the buyers are motivated to increase business with your company to leverage additional benefits?

Decision

When the negotiation phase is over, an agreement is reached, and the selected supplier is informed of the decision. Suppliers who were not selected are usually also informed of the decision.

7) Suppliers' Feedback

The objective of the supplier feedback phase is to explain the decision to the selected and non-selected companies. I often hear from non-selected suppliers that they are surprised when they receive good feedback, which is not all that common. Out of respect to all suppliers who quoted, I believe they deserve appropriate retroaction. There is a tendency to offer more feedback to suppliers who did not get a contract, but selected suppliers should insist on getting feedback to come up even stronger next time with other clients.

When feedback is provided, suppliers should listen and not argue or show frustration toward buyers. A bad attitude is likely to reduce the level of detail provided and to jeopardize future bidding opportunities. Anyway, decisions cannot be reversed at this stage, so it's best to finish on good terms.

There are many challenges for new suppliers, and perhaps the offer was good, but internal stakeholders were not supportive. Or perhaps additional transition costs were discovered during the tender process. While the exact reasons may not always be communicated, the best strategy is to keep all doors open going forward.

Once feedback has been provided and the response is negative, you should state that your company is available and eager to take part in future bidding opportunities. It is a good strategy to conclude by expressing that it must have been difficult to select a proposition, but you appreciate the opportunity that was given and the quality of the feedback. Reassure the buyer and/or budget holder that feedback will be taken into consideration for future bidding opportunities.

When a tender process is lost because a mandate was not perfectly aligned with your company's strengths, you should be sure to communicate what those strengths are. This may entice buyers to invite your company to quote on slightly different projects for which you might be a better fit.

8) Purchase Order / Contract

To confirm an agreement and authorization to pay a supplier, companies generally issue purchase orders. In some companies, the administrative process is quite long and can take a while before the supplier receives a purchase order.

For services or products that cannot wait to be delivered, suppliers may feel the pressure to start working without a purchase order. Although in theory, this should not happen, flexibility may be appreciated.

Before accepting, suppliers should receive a written confirmation from the budget holder (indirect) as a minimum and ideally, from the procurement department. Suppliers should not feel bad about insisting on getting a written confirmation. This is very important because projects could be cancelled while some work has already been carried out. Additionally, running a credit check is a good idea if there are any doubts regarding the client's ability to pay.

For some products or services, a separate contract in addition to a purchase order may be required. Depending on the organization that you are dealing with, contracts can also take a while before they get signed. Sometimes the customer cannot wait for a contract to be signed before receiving products or services. One way of offering flexibility to your customers is through a Letter of Intent (LOI). This document indicates a genuine interest in coming to an agreement and can help to speed-up the process.

It is recommended that suppliers have standard contracts available, as customers may request them. When a potential customer asks to review a standard contract, it is recommended that you make some adjustments prior to sharing, as some clauses can be abusive. For example, charging an 18% interest rate in case of late payment to a big corporation will not be well perceived. Once, during an RFP to acquire printers, I had to challenge a clause about paying for scanning pages. This clause was later removed, but it was quite abusive because companies don't charge for using a scanner on a printer.

Suppliers are advised not to complain about their customer's contractual process. Dealing with large corporations requires extra effort and a lot of follow-ups. Buyers can be good allies with suppliers when dealing with their legal department, but nothing replaces the support from budget holders who need their project to move forward (indirect). What is requested from legal may not always be reasonable, but it can certainly be discussed.

Contracts are written to protect companies and conflicts are rare. Companies do not want to sue their suppliers and will usually compromise when issues arise. In my experience, American companies take contracts very seriously.

Canadian companies are much more flexible. For example, I have never experienced a Canadian supplier complaining about purchase order clauses. In my experience, Canadian suppliers don't even read the small print at the back of purchase orders. On the other hand, American companies usually challenge all POs and contracts. Obviously there are reasons for these precautions.

Once a contract has been awarded, the next step is to perform a performance evaluation.

9) PERFORMANCE EVALUATION

Formal SPM (supplier performance management) reviews are conducted mainly with strategic suppliers. Most of the time, stakeholders do not feel the need for these reviews until they face issues. It is recommended that procurement and budget holders (when procurement is not involved) conduct a yearly performance meeting as a minimum. This would apply to strategic and non-strategic suppliers. As previously mentioned, in the case of non-strategic suppliers, it may be a less formal process where procurement is simply advised of the results.

Some Benefits:

- Allows for improvements on both sides

- Enhances relationships

- Offers additional exposure for new opportunities

- Reduces the likelihood of getting replaced by competitors

- Provides an opportunity to better understand your customers and tailor products and or services

Having seen the complete sourcing process, I will provide some insight on how to potentially reduce the need for your customers to constantly issue RFPs.

STRATEGIES TO REDUCE TENDERS

Answering tenders (RFPs and RFQs) takes time and costs money. Thus, it is in everyone's interest to reduce tender frequencies and strengthen partnerships.

The reason buyers need to issue tenders is to ensure they are getting the best deals and be in a position to demonstrate this to others in the company. When requirements change another tender is generally issued. One way to cope with this challenge is to introduce flexible financial models that could apply to different scenarios.

To clarify, I will provide some examples of what could be done. Remuneration models and strategies have to be adapted for different business contexts.

Consultants

Consultants generally charge hourly rates for different categories of employees through a rate card. In order to cover for future needs, the recommendation is to share a broader range of consultant rates. In addition to predefined rates, an annual volume rebate could be introduced.

To increase the odds of securing additional business, periodically enquiring about new projects helps. The idea is to be present and demonstrate to your customers that they already have a preferred agreement.

If a buyer is faced with additional requests, then he could simply refer to the agreement, instead of having to go back to the market.

Stationary and promotional items

Companies that are selling standard items usually share price lists. Good examples are stationary and promotional items. For these types of products, the ideal would be to share a broad price list so that customers can validate preferential rates. There should be a way for the client to be certain that new items that were not pre identified in that list also benefit from a discount.

Additional fees such as transport, customs etc. should be detailed in the invoices. The agreement should state if these costs are charged at cost or not.

Event Management

Event management companies usually charge a management fee that can be calculated by applying a percentage on overall spending. The services that are included in the management fee should be clearly explained. Those that are booking hotels on behalf of customers usually receive a commission from hotels (IATA members). Stating what the commission is inspires trust. All invoices from third party suppliers should be included in the final bill. Invoices from third party suppliers should be charged at cost. There should not be hidden rebates from third-party suppliers. If there is a mark-up on third-party spending, it should be stated what it is in the commercial agreement. Adding an annual volume discount is also recommended.

The challenge with purchasing events is that costs vary, according to how and where the event is executed. For example, a supplier could have a lower management fee, but always book venues where AV rental is necessary, thus costing more in the end. Suppliers should have discussions with budget holders and buyers so they understand that money is spent wisely.

Offering Options

As we have already briefly covered, giving options to your customers will help them feel they can choose and be involved in the process. Comments, such as "Why have I never been offered this option from my regular supplier?" should be avoided.

I will share a personal selling experience on providing options and giving advice in the customers' best interest.

Years ago, I used to sell chemical products for swimming pools during the summer. There was an entrepreneur, who came to our store regularly and always bought the same products. As it was my job to satisfy customers, I recommended that he buy some of the chemicals in bulk to save on costs. These products were hidden in the warehouse and used mainly by employees. I had expected the entrepreneur to thank me, but instead, he was upset that no one had mentioned it before.

I am sure readers will think that I was too forthcoming, but the founder's prime focus had been on giving good advice to his customers. Customers knew our products were sold at a premium, and many were willing to pay more for good advice. While I understand the dilemma when presented with a choice between making more money and serving customers, the day those customers find out that they could have been better served is the day they may go elsewhere.

As a buyer, I often find different products or services at much lower costs. Every time this happens, we (stakeholders) feel that we have been taken advantage of. To avoid this, always offer customers other options when possible. For instance, if you are selling promotional pens, recommend not only the most expensive model, but also those of various price ranges. This recommendation should be followed, even for customers who have been ordering more expensive pens for five years. Reminding them that there are other options is an important way to maintain trust.

Higher trust can result in fewer RFPs and RFQs and more sole sourcing, which should be your objective!

CHAPTER 4 TAKEAWAYS

The strategic sourcing process explained in this book covers 9 main activities:

1) Needs Identification

The need identification phase is crucial, as it sets the foundations for the following steps. Buyers can gather information from different sources to better understand and explain what is required. Proactive suppliers can facilitate the learning process by interacting with buyers and ideally budget holders.

2) Market Analysis

This phase is about researching and analyzing what the market (suppliers) has to offer. There are different ways for buyers to look for potential suppliers. The web has become a great source of information. To facilitate procurement work, it is essential that procurement is able to reach a sales department easily and quickly; otherwise, the opportunity may be lost.

3) Purchasing Strategies

At this stage, procurement must bring value to the organization and establish how to accomplish objectives. Purchasing strategies must be adapted to each situation with proper internal support in order to bring value.

4) Market Approaches, Mainly RFPs and RFQs

Suppliers may be asked to provide quotations without necessarily going through a rigid sourcing process.

For example, prices can be asked over the phone. When sourcing important purchases over a sourcing limit, large companies are likely to have formal processes and will issue an RFP or an RFQ.

5) Proposal Presentations

Written proposals provide great insight into a supplier's capabilities, but good presentations can influence decision makers. This is especially relevant for service providers.

The evaluation team must sense that the supplier wants to fulfill customer needs. For that reason, it is usually appreciated when suppliers express their gratitude at being asked to participate in a tender process and inform potential customers that they wish to work with them. Obviously, they have to demonstrate that they have what it takes to become the best partner.

6) Suppliers' Selection & Post Tender Negotiations

The selection committee's role is to evaluate which supplier can best fulfill needs at an appropriate cost.

Buyers are usually in a good position to negotiate, because they have probably seen multiple proposals.

Naturally, cost is often not the only criteria, especially when selecting service providers. It is difficult for suppliers to assess if they should add some buffer when quoting. There are no easy answers to this, as it depends on the situation.

7) Supplier's Feedback

Seeking feedback after a tender process is helpful for the future. It is important to be receptive and not argumentative; decisions cannot be reversed at this stage. Thanking the buyer and expressing a strong desire to do future business are good strategies to keep the doors open.

8) Purchase Order/ Contract

Most companies issue purchase orders when contracting with suppliers and often require a contract. When delivering without a purchase order, it is highly recommended validating with procurement first (they should get written confirmation, according to the delegation of authority for their own benefit). Suppliers are advised to have standard contracts available, as large corporations are likely to ask for them.

9) Performance Evaluations

Conducting evaluations with strategic suppliers concludes the strategic sourcing process. Non-strategic suppliers should suggest holding at least an annual review. Another benefit of this exercise is to remind buyers of your existence as they play a referral role.

CHAPTER 5: MANAGING GIFTS AND ENTERTAINMENT

This chapter explains basic rules related to gifts and entertainment.

Gifts and entertainment is a sensitive subject to tackle, as there are so many different business contexts. For example, most people would feel comfortable when a marketing department set up a special expensive program involving activities to thank important customers.

On the other hand, a lot of people think it normal when buyers do not accept gifts as a means of protecting their impartiality. Buyers are usually very sensitive to this subject and may even put their own restrictive rules in place when none exist. For example, they are likely to limit the value of what they can receive, forbid this practice, or draw modest gifts between employees.

The reality is that budget holders (indirect procurement) often have more influence than buyers in sourcing decisions. In an ideal world, companies would have a standard code of business conduct that would apply to all employees. Since it is virtually impossible to provide exact guidelines on the topic, especially when we think of international contexts, I will provide some basic guidelines to avoid missteps.

General Guidelines:

- Buyers should not receive gifts or invitations during RFPs, RFQs, and RFIs.

- Always check with buyers what the rules are in order avoid negative reactions. As rules sometimes change, this can be revisited later.

- Excessive gifts should not be given, as buyers do not want to feel or give the impression that they owe anything.

- A supplier not already dealing with a customer should not give gifts, unless it is a very low value item, such as a pen or a USB key. Inviting a non-customer for lunch is likely to be refused, unless it is a lunch aimed at optimizing time and/or that business is very likely to occur.

- When accepted, gifts that can be shared between employees reach more people and are more transparent. When accepted and appropriate, gifts that can be shared are usually appreciated by people who are working behind the scenes, like accounts payable, legal etc. Building relationships with these people may be useful. For example, if there are payment issues, knowing who to contact always helps.

- When accepted, personal gifts are likely to have more impact.

- When accepted, activities that involve learning about the industry are likely to be appreciated by buyers and may represent a good opportunity to build relationships. It also offers the opportunity to discover the type of interactions that many budget holders are more likely to experience than buyers, and it allows purchasers to better understand the business context.

- When accepted, lunching with buyers offers an opportunity to engage on a different level. When invitations are extended outside of the formal sourcing process, there is a greater chance of it being accepted, while allowing for a more personal connection.

- When accepted, a lunch after a successful sourcing process can be a good way to begin a business relationship.

- Allowing budget holders to meet with suppliers outside of work and not with procurement is definitely not ideal.

CHAPTER 5 TAKEAWAYS

- Because of the importance of budget holders in decision making for indirect categories, sourcing policies on gift and entertainment would ideally also apply to budget holders.

- To avoid missteps when inviting a purchaser for lunch or to participate in an activity, suppliers are recommended to enquire on the customers' gift and entertainment policy.

- Activities that allow sharing sourcing related knowledge with purchasers are usually appreciated and have more chances of being accepted.

Chapter 6 Maintaining Customers

This chapter recaps some of the concrete actions that entrepreneurs and sales representatives can use to retain existing customers.

A statistic from Christine S. Filip, (1994) revealed the importance of keeping existing customers. You need to "find three more customers to replace the original customer, a process that is five to six times more expensive than maintaining an existing relationship." This statistic is an average, but there are certainly some customers that are worth more than others. For this reason, every idea to help keep customers should be examined. Maintaining business over a long period requires constant work and careful management of the relationship.

It is no wonder that suppliers, who take customers for granted, are likely to lose them at some point. When it happens, it does not necessarily mean that a superior supplier has replaced your company; it may only be that your competitors were more proactive in servicing and demonstrating their value.

Maintaining Customers Checklist (Ongoing Relationships)

Defining Needs:

- Leverage your expertise and help customers define what is needed, offer options, and discuss cost drivers. This support will demonstrate a genuine desire to help.

- Support the need definition phase, instead of asking for a budget.

- Enquire about the expected life expectancy of products to come up with appropriate solutions.

- Consider offering free pilots when presenting new ideas; this will allow them to experience something new.

Submitting Prices:

- Provide detailed cost breakdowns (quotes and invoices).

- Suggest options at different prices.

- Make sure that understanding your quotations is a no brainer; for example, clearly identify what is an option and sum up numbers.

- Remain fair when changes are requested to a proposal; modifications do not necessarily mean higher costs.

- Communicate termination penalties well in advance.

- When prospecting new clients, communicate that it is always a pleasure to provide quotations and that it does not entail an obligation.

- Suggest a remuneration model to procurement/budget holders that could be used for several orders. Ask what can be done to reduce RFPs frequency.

Timeline:

- Acknowledge receipt of customers' requests.

- Clarify with customers an appropriate lead-time to respond to queries.

- Inform customers in advance when there is a risk for a late delivery.

- Whenever a customer asks for modifications, communicate and agree on timeline impacts.

- Remain punctual, even if your customers are always late for meetings.

- If one of your sales representative is leaving, allow for an appropriate transition time to prevent disruptions to your customers.

Savings:

- Proactively suggest saving opportunities.

- Track savings from third party suppliers; this can help secure better rates for your services.

- Try to accommodate customers asking for better prices. Think of other ways to reduce cost while mutually benefiting from it.

- Advertise special discounts on all invoices and quotations and communicate and demonstrate that there is a strong partnership.

- Support buyers in calculating savings.

- Visit customers when it is time to discuss annual volume rebates.

Supplier Performance Reviews:

- Recommend regular meetings to review performance.

- Suggest KPIs to ease the process and make sure to involve procurement (including for indirect categories where procurement is not always involved).

- When there are issues, acknowledge problems and fix them as soon as possible.

Building Relationships:

- Get seen by visiting customers, instead of using the phone.

- Be organized; answering phone calls without having to leave a message is always appreciated.

- Ask from time to time if there are new employees in the department and offer to introduce yourself.

- Acknowledge the importance of your customers.

- Help when necessary, even when requirements are out of scope.

- Be willing to fix issues, even if they were caused by the client.

- Inform customers when refusing to deal with competitors. Ask for permission when in doubt (highly appreciated!)

- Show a good attitude towards buyers and seek their involvement. They have a referral role and can definitely help secure business.

- Always remain professional and polite with all stakeholders.

- When answering a tender from a long-time customer, invest as much energy as you would if it was a new customer.

- Never complain when a quotation does not result in an order or when a project has been cancelled.

- When an order is lost, be polite and enquire as to the reasons without reacting negatively.

- Enquire about your customer's gift and entertainment policy.

- Meet with buyers, especially when there's nothing to be gained.

- Organize office visits to educate your potential and regular customers.

- Build a personal website for your important customers, which displays products that can be ordered, as well as a forum for receiving and sharing customer feedback.

- Explain to customers all that is done to avoid issues and reduce risks.

Process Optimization

- Enquire about your customer's internal processes to assess what could be improved, thanks to your dedication.

- Help your customers by taking on consuming administrative tasks and become an extension of your important customers.

- Inform customers of internal constraints; this allows them to understand why better planning may be required.

- Clarify roles and responsibilities, suggest improvements.

- Ensure that samples left always have your contact info on them; this will facilitate ordering.

Confidentiality:

- Make sure that no sensitive information about other customers is shared; this would leave a bad impression.

*Some of the actions listed can also apply to other stages of the relationship.

Conclusion

As we have seen throughout the book, selling to large corporations is complex, and the selling/sourcing context is in constant evolution. If you are the owner of a company or a sales representative, you are likely to face different challenges with different customers. You may be lucky and rely on repetitive business, have to constantly answer bid requests, struggle to bid and/or win tenders, or suddenly have to deal with procurement. Even if you are in a comfortable position and rely on good products or services, new challenges are likely to pop up.

One thing is certain; being proactive and knowledgeable certainly can help gain and retain customers. What needs to be remembered is that selling to large corporations requires that you not only focus on your products and/or services, but on making sure that buyers and budget holders (when relevant) have all the elements they need to understand why they should feel comfortable buying from your company. Customers should also be reminded of your presence, especially when dealing with companies that have high turnover.

In general, suppliers are more knowledgeable about their products and services than customers are, since it is their main focus. For this reason, the expertise should definitely be exploited and shared appropriately. By developing a better relationship with procurement, you are more likely to have the opportunity to engage on a deeper level and manage to become collaborative partners.

In other words, you should not fear dealing with procurement.

If you are a buyer, you are also likely to face many challenges, especially if you focus on indirect categories where buyers have traditionally been less involved than with direct procurement. What buyers need to remember is that their objective is similar to those of suppliers, to fulfill the internal customer needs, while keeping in mind that the company expects enhanced value. As a buyer, you may have a lot of freedom when it comes to finding ways to add value. The essential thing to remember is that suppliers can participate in this mission, especially if you focus on the big picture and not only on price.

I sincerely hope that you have appreciated this examination of the procurement world and that the knowledge I have shared can help make you be more successful.

Thank you for choosing to read this book. If you also have expertise to share, I encourage you to do so!

APPENDICES

APPENDIX 1: PROS AND CONS OF NEGOTIATING WITH OR WITHOUT A BUDGET HOLDER

Pros:

Negotiating and meeting suppliers without budget holders	Negotiating and meeting suppliers with a budget holder
Faster	Expertise can be shared
Less opportunity to communicate information that could limit negotiations (example: providing a budget or demonstrating too much enthusiasm)	Less chance that important information is forgotten
Less opportunity to leak non-verbal information	Improved buy-in as budget holders participate in the supplier's selection
	Helpful when the budget is limited; budget holders can definitely add pressure during negotiations

Figure 20

Cons:

Negotiating and meeting suppliers without budget holders	Negotiating and meeting suppliers with a budget holder
Can limit budget holder's engagement	Longer process when many stakeholders are involved
Higher chance for complaints, as budget holders have played a lesser role in the selection process	Important information that can limit negotiation can be communicated, sometimes without realizing it (misalignment)
Important information can be missing	
Less support in generating good ideas	
Note: Some organizations require that two people assist during negotiations (can reduce conflict of interest perception, or provide a witness in case of issues). This second person is not necessarily a budget holder.	

Figure 21

APPENDIX 2: ADVANTAGES AND DISADVANTAGES FOR BUYERS OR BUDGET HOLDERS TO PROVIDE BUDGETS

Providing Budgets:

Advantages	Disadvantages
Faster to source, what is presented fits the budget	Possibility of getting overcharged (paying more than what it is worth)
Less important to provide clear requirements as the project can start right away	Possibility of unnecessary spending (buying more than necessary)
Less chance of exceeding the budget	Fewer options, there could be good ideas from lower-cost options
	Less likely to lead to a good understanding of what has to be sourced, which can lead to budget holders' dissatisfaction

Figure 22

Not Providing Budgets

Advantages	Disadvantages
More options are likely to be presented	When quotes exceed budget, more back and forth with suppliers may be required
Easier to negotiate as different solutions can be provided	Possibility that budget is insufficient, thus cancelling or delaying projects when a lot of work has already been done
Less chance of paying more than the true value	

Figure 23

APPENDIX 3: RECOMMENDED ATTITUDE WHEN SUDDENLY DEALING WITH PROCUREMENT

This section covers the recommended attitude for entrepreneurs and sales representatives when they suddenly have to deal with procurement, instead of working directly with budget holders.

When procurement gets in the way, the reaction from existing suppliers is likely to be negative, as they generally fear that procurement will only look at costs, run RFPs and RFQs, and that buyers will not take into consideration all that is done to satisfy customers.

When a procurement function is new, buyers are also likely to struggle to collaborate with budget holders. This reality should not signal an opportunity to join this resistance, as eventually, buyers will earn their place. Potential suppliers constantly solicit buyers; procurement may become motivated to explore alternatives if they feel a lack of collaboration.

The right attitude includes respecting procurement, collaborating with them, and making sure they understand your value. If procurement is not in a position to understand the additional value that a supplier brings, they are not likely to take unknown elements into consideration.

There is a greater chance that procurement understands the value of long-term suppliers when they witness how valuable they are. This can be achieved by spending time with buyers to explain what your company is offering, the expertise it has developed over the years, and the personalized service that is offered.

Ideally, when buyers can experience the service, it helps them to understand the value. For example, if your company sells products or services, an office visit combined with a field visit (when relevant) helps to demonstrate what is delivered and how well it is done.

Let's not fool ourselves; demonstrating expertise, customer knowledge, and explaining the quality of the product or service will not be enough to stop procurement from doing its job. The only way for procurement to ensure working with reliable and competitive suppliers is to perform sourcing processes.

A company may decide to switch suppliers, perhaps in order to reduce cost. When this happens, there is also a slight chance that the customer realizes it made a mistake. Keeping a good attitude helps regain customers. There is also the possibility that the new supplier is far superior.

APPENDIX 4: BUILDING A VALUE PROPOSITION

This additional section provides guidance to sales professionals when introducing their company to potential customers. Buyers will gain some insight on researching suppliers.

Existing Customers

Entrepreneurs and sales representatives may wonder what to tell prospective customers in order to generate interest in their products or services. A good way to find out is to enquire from long-term existing customers. Existing customers can be informed that you are looking at expanding your business, and that you would like their input in understanding what they appreciate most when dealing with your company. When selling a service, it may be necessary to reassure existing customers that expanding will not affect the quality of their service. If necessary, examples of how many customers you have managed to work with simultaneously can be provided. Receiving verbal feedback is good, but recommendation letters from customers are powerful marketing tools that can be utilised in many circumstances. For example, they can be shared when responding to RFPs or RFQs, posted on your corporate websites, and forwarded to prospective customers.

Advising a good customer that you are looking at expanding your business may generate interest in supporting your initiative. For example, a buyer may share references of suppliers or other buyers requiring similar products or services. With a bit of luck, a buyer could also introduce your company directly to other potential customers.

In addition to buyers, I also recommend asking budget holders (services) for feedback, since they are likely to have an appreciation for different areas of your business because of their different focus. They may also suggest other potential clients.

New Company

If you have recently launched a company, asking what existing customers appreciate about your offer will most likely not be possible. Prospecting customers should then be seen as an opportunity to confirm interest in your products and/or services and tailor your offering and approach.

This enquiry is part of the process that I had followed for this book. I targeted specific key readers who I believed would benefit from this book (buyers, entrepreneurs, sales representatives, consultants, purchasing associations, and recent business graduates). With persistence, I managed to find professionals who were willing to participate in the feedback process. I discovered that professionals from the sales side unanimously appreciated my book, though there were enhancements required to make it more useful to a broader range of business professionals.

Demonstrating Expertise

Whether a company specializes in manufacturing products or selling services, a value proposition should incorporate personal strengths. When you buy a service, you indirectly buy the people delivering them. When you buy products, you also buy services associated with those products. A good way to explain your strengths and expertise is by providing examples of how you have served other customers.

For instance, an event supplier once explained that he had to shovel a mountain of sand as a result of road construction work because it was blocking an entrance guests needed to enter a building. I had the sense the story was real because the employee expressed emotion while describing his experience.

Building a value proposition (establishing what you have to offer) helps when contacting potential customers and this information is useful to share on websites, when cold calling, meeting with potential customers, and when sharing knowledge with purchasers.

Websites

As day-to-day customers, most of us enjoy surfing the web for our online shopping needs. Surprisingly, a lot of small companies don't have websites, and even those who are experts, such as web companies, probably spend little time on their websites. Websites can be used to find out about your company and to jump-start discussions when prospecting.

From a buyer's perspective, I will share what I consider important when searching suppliers online. Firstly, when a buyer is looking at acquiring a product or a service, he must be able to find it close by and quickly. Buyers feel more secure buying from suppliers who are closer to their office, or at least in the same city. This makes face-to-face meetings with suppliers simpler and buyers won't regret that a supplier had to travel long distances when they are only exploring the supply market.

To find suppliers quickly, it is important that relevant keywords are associated with your products or services. Companies are likely to use different terminology, so confirming which keywords existing customers would use to locate your company is a good idea. In addition, there are companies specializing in boosting web traffic that can provide valuable recommendations.

Secondly, value propositions can be made more compelling and realistic by adding images and videos. If you have a nice factory or office, adding pictures increases credibility. However, posting images can be tricky, as buyers are looking for a match. To maximize the chances of a match, I recommend that the images be segregated into different categories. For example, if you are an event management company that has posted pictures of high-end events, then you may have categorized your company as specializing in higher cost events. Being wrongly categorized may reduce opportunities to work on smaller mandates or vice versa.

Thirdly, recommendations from major clients are extremely valuable. It is better to display references from repeat customers on your website, rather than references from one-time clients. Always ask for permission before posting feedback.

Fourth, a good website should allow easy communication with companies. Surprisingly, getting in touch with potential suppliers is not always straightforward. Even when you managed to locate a phone number on a website, getting through to the right department can be timely and difficult. After talking to an employee, you may be redirected to someone else.

The worst scenario is when a potential customer is only able to get in touch via an online request form, with responses not being made regularly.

When a corporate buyer is looking for new suppliers, he needs to be able to reach sales quickly. When calling multiple companies, those that cannot be reached easily risk getting discarded. As a buyer and a day-to-day customer, I am always impressed when I need technical support from Apple or my Internet provider. They have a request form that you complete online, and two minutes later someone calls you. This is also what corporate buyers hope for.

In my opinion, restricting customers to communicating electronically is a bad investment decision. It does not provide customers with the opportunity for direct conversation with a competent sales employee. Pre-qualifying suppliers for next steps can be done quite rapidly.

BUILDING A VALUE PROPOSITION SUMMARY

- Entrepreneurs and private companies need to develop a compelling value proposition. For existing companies, it is recommended asking for feedback from existing customers.

- For a new company, prospecting new customers should also be seen as a good opportunity to understand what potential customers are looking to find.

- Most buyers from North America research suppliers on the web. To facilitate their research, it is recommended that your website has been optimised for search engines and that it is indexed using the right key words for your industry. Businesses should ideally confirm these key words with existing and potential customers, as each company is likely to have different jargon.

- When buyers are researching potential suppliers on the web, they expect to have enough information to assess if the company could be a good fit. In order to avoid being wrongly categorized, it is important to illustrate through explanations, pictures, videos, and testimonials from a wide range of customers.

- Recommendation letters or testimonials should be posted on the company's website. Buyers feel reassured when they see that other important customers are satisfied.

- It should be easy for buyers to find sales contact information and communicate by phone. Consulting a website does provide some information, but nothing replaces speaking to a knowledgeable person; first impressions are very important. The person who answers the phone should have the answers.

APPENDIX 5: PROSPECTING

This bonus section explains how to become more effective when prospecting potential customers. Sales professionals will learn what questions can be asked to better assess business potential and the reason persistence in acquiring new customers can sometimes pay off. Purchasers will get to understand the challenges that sales professionals face when prospecting new customers.

Targeting Companies

Direct Procurement:

From experience, direct buyers will not spend long hours looking for manufacturing product ads in magazines or on the web. In fact, they are not likely to do that at all. Buyers are more likely to be searching for companies on the web and meeting with sales representatives who have contacted them.

To identify what a company might be interested in buying, sales representatives can usually leverage industrial databases that are more tailored for direct acquisitions. Once a company is identified as a potential customer, the next step would be getting in touch with procurement to evaluate business potential and to set up a timely meeting.

Indirect Procurement:

Figuring out which indirect category a company is acquiring is more challenging. Industry databases are more relevant for direct, rather than indirect purchases. A strategy to figure out what a company is buying is to look for buyers' job descriptions from targeted companies and consult LinkedIn buyers' curriculum vitaes. A follow up phone call usually allows you to confirm information quickly.

Personal Connections:

When entrepreneurs or sales representatives know someone working for a potential customer, it is a good idea to ask this person to provide the procurement contact information. Knowing someone from the inside may help to secure a meeting and get a call back. However, it is important to assess business potential over the phone, so as to avoid unnecessary meetings that may be arranged out of politeness.

Contacting Potential Customers by Phone:

Why are entrepreneurs and sales representatives calling buyers and budget holders?

The answer that probably comes to mind is to make a sale.

The right answers are:

- To evaluate business potential
- To assess compatibility between companies
- To eventually deliver products and/or services

- As an extra, enjoy pleasant business relationships

Prospecting calls should not be seen as a psychologically difficult process where rejection is the norm. It should be used to assess if further effort is worthwhile, to gain insight into the customer and/or industry's needs, and to understand how to potentially get a foot in the door.

When speaking to a buyer, there is no need to oversell your company. Being professional, articulate, and able to answer questions is what the corporate buyer is looking for. If there is no interest, there is no need to push it. However, it is important to call back until contact is established. Most of the time, prospecting suppliers call a couple of times and then stop if there is no response. The reality is that when the buyer is busy and there is no urgent need, there is a good chance that the buyers won't call back.

Assessing Business Potential:

Just because a potential customer buys similar products and/or services to those you are offering does not mean there are good chances of selling to that customer. You will find areas to be explored in order to assess business potential:

- Is the potential customer used to tender new projects?

- Is the potential customer mainly dealing with the same suppliers?

- Is annual spending significant enough for buyers/ budget holders to be interested in a potential sourcing process?

- Is the potential customer bound by an exclusivity agreement for a certain period?

- Is the potential customer currently unsatisfied with its existing supplier?

- Is the potential customer interested in benchmarking costs and possibly achieving savings?

- Is the potential customer interested in identifying back-up suppliers to reduce supply risks?

- Is the potential customer working with a competitor who has less to offer?

- Is the buyer interested in learning about specific products, services and/or the industry?

Prospecting Call Example:

Here is an example of what a prospecting phone call could look like.

"Hello, my name is X. I am working for X. I would like to know who I should contact to introduce my products or services (that you will most likely explain briefly)."

You should be able to get the contact information from a receptionist. If reaching the procurement department is not possible, try contacting customer service. In theory, it should be easier to reach and they can probably provide buyers' contact information. I recommend calling in between hours, as the buyer is less likely to have meetings or other obligations. If there is no answer, leave a message and follow-up.

Leaving a Message:

"Hi Mister X, my name is X. I am calling on behalf of X, and we specialize in X. I believe that our product/ service could be of interest to your company, and I would like to touch base with you to evaluate. You can reach me at XX, thank you."

If you are lucky, you may get a call back; if not, try again. Gradually increase the time between phone calls to avoid appearing pushy. If you don't hear back from procurement, but know that business potential exists, try reaching a budget holder or another buyer.

A buyer answers the phone

"Hi Mister X, it is great to speak with you. I am working for X and would like to take a moment to introduce our company. Before doing so, I'd like to enquire if you are the person responsible for buying X."

If your company is working for well-known companies, include this during your discussion and explain why you believe you could bring value. Some relevant questions are as follows:

Possible Interaction Topics When Business Potential Exists:

- Have you been in charge of sourcing this product/service for a long time? (Assessing buyer experience and potential to share category expertise.)

- We have managed to improve efficiency with similar customers; I would welcome the opportunity to present what was accomplished. Maybe it could apply to your company.

- We have a new product or service to introduce. Would it be possible to send you some information by e-mail with our web link? (You could use the opportunity to attach recommendation letters from similar customers, but not necessarily competitors).

- Would you like to learn about the industry? There is no obligation to buy, and it allows me the opportunity to introduce our company, which is part of my job!

- Do you usually run quotation processes or deals with the same suppliers?

- I would welcome the opportunity to quote without obligation; this would allow you to evaluate whether your current suppliers are competitive.

When there is an interest to meet with your company, the next step is to schedule a meeting. Nowadays, introductory meetings can be facilitated through the web, although face-to-face presentations are generally preferable, but not always possible. When scheduling a meeting with a buyer, it is a good practice to ask if other people (i.e. budget holder, users etc.) can also attend.

Good Suppliers Already in Place

When buyers express satisfaction with current suppliers, I would recommend asking what it is that they like most about their supplier.

Example:

"Mister X, I understand the situation, and I have a lot of respect for buyers who value their existing relationships. Would you mind sharing what you like most about your existing supplier? I would really like to understand what a big corporation such as yours, requires?"

This type of information allows suppliers to understand what it means for that company to be a good or exceptional supplier. This may open the door for further discussions or simply provide insight for future reference. In the event that your company could be a good fit, but an exceptional supplier is already in place, you can always mention that a back-up plan may be helpful and getting a quote is free and entails no obligations.

Unnecessary Pressure

Unlike personal purchases that can be postponed more easily, buyers make purchases because there are internal requests to respond to. For this reason, it is not necessary to put pressure (closing tactics) when selling to a company. What buyers want is to rationally evaluate what is presented.

An effective strategy to earn and maintain business is to demonstrate commitment to serving customers and make their lives worry free. The minute that buyers and budget holders perceive that a potential supplier's goal is mainly to get new business and not serve the customer, they will lose interest. The focus must be on fulfilling a need with passion and dedication, rather than making the sale.

Getting a Foot in the Door Through Non-Core Services

All companies have core products/services that they sell. Naturally, companies focus on their main revenue stream to attract customers. The problem with this focus is that it can lead to situations where some customers may not understand everything that is available to them. Offering and communicating a wide range of products or services usually enhances selling opportunities and opens the door to selling core product and services.

As an example, we once met with a supplier who we all loved. Unfortunately for the sales representative, our current supplier was so reliable and competitive that we would not have considered doing business with another company at that point. Although the sales representative had a core business, his company offered other non-core services which he made clear. A year after meeting with that supplier, I was looking for big, plastic envelopes and having a hard time sourcing these. The sales representatives had made such a good impression and had advised us that he could get anything, I called him and he managed to find the product.

Small transactions are important because once a supplier is created in a purchasing system, future purchases become easier.

Limited Opportunities Due to Internal Resistance

New suppliers generally have a harder time getting a foot in the door due to internal resistance from budget holders and many additional variables. I recognize the challenge, but it is important to know that business context evolves. I have listed a series of events that can facilitate hiring new suppliers.

Business Context Evolving:

- Budget holders and or buyers rotate positions

- New procurement rules with sourcing limits that require competitive tenders

- Budget pressure

- Personal contacts make it easier to communicate with decision makers

- Buyers/budget holders recognize that there are superior suppliers available

- Buyers/budget become open to look for change or simply test the market

- A supplier screwed-up or faced bankruptcy

Prospecting Past Customers:

Nowadays, it is quite rare for a supplier to keep its customers for extended periods of time. Depending on the reasons a customer/contract was lost, it may be possible to secure new business again. Sometimes, new suppliers are hired but may not turn out as expected.

One of the keys to winning business back is to get as much feedback as possible when a contract is lost. Buyers may be inclined to provide insight if suppliers show genuine interest without displaying discontent. Sometimes, the real reasons cannot be communicated at the time. For example, it would be awkward for me to say that poor service influenced the decision. This would likely be followed up with a question, such as **"then why did you ask for a quote if we had no chance?"** To avoid dealing with this, buyers may choose not to communicate the real issues. Buyers prefer to keep all options available, because they never know the outcome of a sourcing process.

It is possible that the supplier who had service issues, is hired again because of significant price differences, less superior options, or he may be the only one satisfying requirements.

The best strategy to avoid dissatisfaction with your customers is prevention. As mentioned earlier, seeking feedback from time to time, or creating a formal supplier performance assessment is recommended. This process can be facilitated by procurement. Another method to seek feedback is to be proactive prior to receiving another quotation opportunity. For example, if your company lost a contract and the next bidding opportunity is in six months, it would be a good idea to get in touch with procurement ASAP. Waiting for the next formal sourcing process to start may limit buyer accessibility, as they have to remain fair and provide similar information to all suppliers. Booking a meeting when there is no urgent need to source can be done by informing buyers of new products/services or to introduce a new sales representative etc. If past service issues are mentioned during that meeting, there will still be a couple of months left to demonstrate what has changed and to come back in due course with statistics to reassure customers.

If your company had service issues that were not communicated or addressed, the next tender process may only serve to make other suppliers more competitive. Ethical buyers should not communicate other suppliers' prices, but the mere fact of adding competition in a tender process is likely to impact outcomes. When responding to a tender request, it is important that suppliers start on the same footing in terms of service expectations and in understanding customers' needs.

Strategies to regain past customers lost due to unreasonable prices, service issues, superior competitors and relationships issues are available below.

Regaining Past Customers

In the following chart, I share possible actions that can be undertaken when losing contracts or customers under different probable scenarios.

	Probability of getting business back			
Reasons for losing contracts:	Low	Medium	High	Possible actions
Unreasonable price		X		Being more competitive, trade business advice that overcompensates for higher prices or in exchange for longer-term commitments. If needed, demonstrate that the business model has changed.
Service issues		X		Understanding and fixing issues, communicating action plans and results prior to new bidding opportunities. Establish frequent meetings to track performance and enhance communications.
Superior competitors	X			Asking for input and assess if changes are possible.
Relationship issues		X		Inform buyer when new employees are taking over the lost account.

Figure 24

You will find below additional explanations for less self-explanatory scenarios.

Unreasonable Prices

For greedy suppliers, the only thing that can help is having specific knowledge or capabilities that competitors don't have. Buyers may decide to maintain a business relationship with such suppliers, because they don't know when they may need them again. In the long run, this is not necessarily the best position.

In the event that a customer has been complaining a lot about price and that orders are down unexpectedly, it would probably be a good idea to enquire as to why this is and change strategy.

Under such circumstances, the supplier should inform buyers if their business model has changed. Buyers will need to witness progress before considering this supplier for further opportunities.

Monetizing Expertise

We all agree that price is an important factor. Unfortunately, focusing too much on cost is not necessarily the best strategy for buyers, as it is possible to save more when teaming up with suppliers. Depending on the situation, it would not be unfair for suppliers to take advantage of their expertise when it can benefit their customers.

For example, in my previous job, an electrical cable supplier offered to spend time with our engineers to optimize electrical cables. This supplier's advice resulted in more than a million dollars in savings. I was told this story when running a quotation between this supplier and another one. As I was new at the time, I was quite impressed and asked if this supplier received special treatment in exchange. The answer was no.

Suppliers who know how to save their customers more than they would get via a tendering process deserve to receive some benefits. If the knowledge means they secure a contract for a reasonable amount of time, then something is provided in return.

If the knowledge only leads them to secure a short-term benefit, it would be wise to negotiate something more in return.

For example, a supplier could provide an estimated number of hours and usual cost required to perform such an analysis on an element of the business. The idea here is to give a value to the consulting service, so it can be considered a saving. In addition, the benefits should also be estimated and traded. For instance, a two-year contract could be negotiated, instead of only one year. I am not saying that all advice should be paid for, but when it results in significant gains, it should be rewarded.

Better Suppliers

When a superior supplier replaces another supplier, it is difficult to get a customer back. However, it is important to understand why this supplier is better and to evaluate if and how the situation could be improved.

Companies that offer more than one main product or service have an advantage. Customers may need something else from you that the other superior supplier doesn't provide. This presents an opportunity to regain business and compare service.

It is important to know that deciding to award business to a supplier when a tender process is not mandatory is not always a purely rational decision. For smaller purchases, buyers or stakeholders may call the supplier they like most.

Prospecting Is a Continuous Effort

Prospecting customers is not only about looking for new customers, but about reminding existing customers of a supplier's existence.

There are many opportunities to do so, and it is important because there is always competition, and the people you are dealing with (clients) are likely to switch positions in large organizations. Employee rotation could mean losing business if other employees don't think of you.

Some suggested actions to reduce the likelihood of getting replaced by another supplier are provided below:

- Ask from time to time if there are new employees in the department and offer to introduce yourself.

- Get seen by visiting customers every so often, instead of using the phone.

- When gifts are accepted, offer a department gift, such as a cake, and take the opportunity to include your company name and what it does.

PROSPECTING SUMMARY

- Industry databases can be leveraged to identify potential customers (more relevant for direct purchases). Companies' job postings or professional business networks, such as LinkedIn can facilitate identifying what indirect buyers acquire. The best way to confirm is to make phone calls.

- When an RFP or RFQ is lost, it is important to know the reasons in order to be better positioned for the next opportunity. Sometimes, the real reasons a proposal was not accepted may not be provided following the quotation process, but it may be possible to investigate at a later date. If this validation is not performed, the next RFP is likely to be lost before it has even started.

- Personal contacts should definitely be leveraged because it helps to get responses.

- When good suppliers are already in place, getting a foot in the company will be harder. Offering to spend time with a buyer to share information on products, services, the industry, what to be careful about etc. may be accepted and can open doors gradually.

- When selling to private companies, putting pressure to gain new business or close a deal is not recommended, unless there are time constraints that could impact a customer's deadline (buyers should be informed of the situation).

- It is important to remember that there are situations that would lead a company to deal with new suppliers. For this reason, it is important to perform periodic follow-ups when business potential exists.

BACK COVER

This book is tailored for professionals, who are looking at improving outcomes in sales and procurement of services. The author, an expert in indirect procurement with more than 10 years of professional experience, will reveal hard-earned secrets to both sellers and purchasers.

Sales professionals, who are willing to venture into the procurement world, will get an edge to allow them to deal more effectively with current and prospective customers. For example, this book covers:

- How suppliers can manage to compete with competitors already in a relationship with their prospective clients.

- How to influence the outcome of an RFP, without sacrificing too much profit.

- How to leverage the procurement function and be the suppliers that receive new business with fewer RFPs to respond to.

Purchasers that are new to acquiring services will understand the dynamics and processes associated with sourcing indirect categories. For example, this knowledge will allow understanding:

- How purchasers can manage to get accepted by budget holders and improve sourcing coverage through value added services.

- How buyers and suppliers can cope with internal resistance that often occurs when new suppliers are invited to compete in RFPs.

- How collaboration between purchasers and suppliers can usually bring more value than the traditional procurement approach of focusing too much on price.

For the cost of this book you will get a head start, receive valuable insights, and enter into successful negotiations much faster. Download now and see the difference inside knowledge will make for you.

ENDNOTES

1. KPMG's European Business Leader Survey. (2011). The Power of Procurement, A Global survey of Procurement functions, p.65.

2. Procurement Leaders. (2013). Procurement planning 2013 part II category planning guide.

3. Proxima,.(2012). Enhancing and redefining the role of indirect procurement-research findings and results, part 2: Why do businesses struggle with effectively managing indirect procurement, p.7.

4. Proxima,.(2012). Direct v indirect procurement, Market intelligence survey, p.5.

5. ANA survey research. (2013). Elevating the Role of Marketing Procurement

6. ANA survey research. (2014). Optimizing the Procurement and Marketing Relationship

7. KPMG's European Business Leader Survey. (2011). The Power of Procurement, A Global survey of Procurement functions, p.3

8. Quotation from Yan Bergeron, Sales Director, PixMob Middle East Africa Turkey

9. KPMG's European Business Leader Survey. (2011). The Power of Procurement, A Global survey of Procurement functions, p.3

10. CAPS Research.(2012).Cross-Industry report of standard benchmarks

11. Ivalua, Spend Management solution provider.(2013). Procurement Executives Survey, Sustained Value Growth vs. Short Therm Cost Reductions: Tracking Procurement Contribution To Corporate Global Performance, p.7.

12. ANA survey research. (2013). Elevating the Role of Marketing Procurement

13. http://www.portal.state.pa.us/portal/server.pt/community/rfp_scoring_formulas_overview/20124, retrieved on August 23,2014

Made in the USA
San Bernardino, CA
19 January 2017